Finance and the Common Good

FINANCE *AND THE* COMMON GOOD

Edited by
Cor van Beuningen &
Kees Buitendijk

Amsterdam University Press

The publication of this book is made possible by grants from The Goldschmeding Chair (Vrije Universiteit, Amsterdam), Templeton World Charity Foundation, Inc. & De Stichting Dr. Abraham Kuyper Fonds

Cover illustration: "Map of the Beemster Polder, Lucas Jansz. Sinck (1664). From the collection of the Dutch National Maritime Museum (Scheepvaartmuseum)."
Cover design: Michiel van Veluwen
Lay-out: Michiel van Veluwen

ISBN   978 94 6372 791 4
NUR   784

Table of Contents

Recommendation   7
By Wopke Hoekstra

Introduction – Finance and the Common Good   10
By Kees Buitendijk and Cor van Beuningen

The Socires Approach - Finance, State, Society   18
By Jos van Gennip

Part 1: Finance and Financialisation

Looking Back at the Banking Crisis: Did We Learn Anything?   31
By Wouter Bos

Financialisation: on Price, Value, Rules and Behaviour   37
By Dirk Bezemer

Why an Open Dialogue is Needed   49
By Eelke de Jong

Complexity, Culture, and Bank Privatisations   60
By Roland Kupers

On the Economic Trinity   69
By Govert Buijs

Part 2: Finance and Relations

Finance: A Relational Perspective   79
By Lans Bovenberg

It's all about us   97
By Cor van Beuningen and Kees Buitendijk

Is Relational Thinking Wishful Thinking?   114
By Johan Graafland

Will Ethics Ever Trump Finance?   122
By Christiaan Vos

Part 3: Relational Finance: Regulation, Policies, Practice

Reconnecting Finance and Society - About Rules and Purpose   133
By Theodor Kockelkoren

Restoring Trust   138
By Sylvester Eijffinger

Pension Funds for the Common Good   143
By Carla Moonen

A Broad Approach to Finance and the Common Good   148
By Steven Vanackere

Part 4: Relational Finance in the World of Tomorrow

Ethics of FinTech: The Need for a Normative Debate
Before the Computer Says 'No'   155
By Maarten Biermans

A European Response to Digitalisation and Globalisation   162
By Haroon Sheikh

Finance, State, and Society in Europe   172
By Herman Van Rompuy

The Global Agenda, the New Economy, and Integrity:
Towards a Sustainable Financial Sector   181
By Jan Peter Balkenende

Fintech and the Common Good   186
By Rens van Tilburg

Concluding remarks   197
By Kees Buitendijk & Cor van Beuningen

About the Contributors   201

Recommendation

By Wopke Hoekstra

Dear reader,

I T IS AN honour to me to recommend to you the important contributions that have been compiled in this publication. I appreciate the efforts of Socires and its partners to broaden and deepen the debate about our financial sector and their quest for a more resilient system. A financial system that is less prone to risks, to boom-and-bust cycles, less debt-driven, and more geared towards long term value creation. Its vital importance to our society, our economy and even our culture deserves such an approach and effort.

In the past forty years, and especially in the aftermath of the 2007-2009 crises, we have witnessed a growing and fundamental imbalance in the relationships between finance, state and society. After the crisis, several measures were taken to restore the health of the financial sector. For example, capital buffers have been strengthened, there are new agreements on bail-in and we introduced the supervision of the product development process. These and other improvements are the result of stricter rules and requirements by the legislator and the regulators, but partly also of initiatives taken by the sector itself, such as introducing disciplinary law in the banking sector.

That, I would say, is a sign of good work towards a more serviceable financial sector as well as a more resilient sector. Still, we have to be alert on problems that might occur and we must be better equipped to reduce the damage to society when they do occur.

And still, we can ask, has the financial sector fully managed to regain the confidence of society? The answer is: no. Despite all the measures taken, in the end it is also a challenge for the sector itself to show that the culture has really changed, that they, for example, do not abuse information advantage on the customer, or that they no longer pass on risks to the taxpayer. It is important that the sector itself takes the lead in restoring trust in financial institutions. This means that the sector does not only act on laws and regulations, but also develops initiatives to create standards that are convincingly suited to social expectations and that they are independently accountable for realizing these standards.

As indicated by the Financial Stability Committee, the European Systemic Risk Board and the European Central Bank, the present atmosphere in the financial markets is not without risks. Because of the relatively loose monetary policy and the global economic recovery there is an almost euphoric mood in the financial markets. This is reflected in low volatility and rising asset prices. Low volatility however can give a distorted picture of the risks. From past experience we know, that it is those quiet periods that imbalances build up. Therefore, as the saying goes, we have to 'fix the roof while the sun is out'.

When market sentiment suddenly changes, for example due to unexpected geopolitical events or a faster than expected monetary exit, sharp price corrections in the financial markets may ensue. The Dutch financial sector is also vulnerable to this, for example through losses on investment portfolios or through pension funds and insurance companies, or via refinancing risks of banks.

In our daily operation, bankers, entrepreneurs and politicians have different responsibilities. Each one of us has its own tasks assigned. But on a higher level, we share the responsibility for the wellbeing of our society and for passing on a beautiful and resilient society to the next generations. That is why this concept of a European, or Rhinelandic arrangement in the triangle of Finance, State and Society is spot on.

We can't leave this discussion to the financial sector alone, or to politics, let alone to just those critics from outside who do not contribute to a viable sustainable alternative for a long time ahead of us. Because that is what we need and that is where our reflections and dialogue should be about: the question whether we are followers in this debate - or can we take the lead, preferably on the basis of inspiration and values, which are at the core of own, identifiable European convictions and values.

I wish you every success in your efforts to develop such an approach in finding a new balance between the interests of the sector, the economy as a whole, the society, the common good and the fostering of a broad,

Recommendation

at least European partnership for the implementation of the sustainable development goals, as is also laid down in the current Coalition Agreement of this Cabinet.

Introduction – Finance and the Common Good

By Kees Buitendijk and Cor van Beuningen

IN HIS VISIONARY cultural study, *The Philosophy of Money* (1900), philosopher and sociologist Georg Simmel states: 'Life teaches us all about money; money teaches us all about life'. Simmel's thesis is that anyone seeking to understand modern society should study the phenomenon of money, and vice versa. As we, in this book, try to understand life in relation to money, or, more specific, to understand what happened *to* and *through* finance in modern society, Simmel gives us a proper first stepping stone; a discourse for understanding the deep cultural embeddedness of our money – and the financial sector. Before we introduce both the aims of this publication and our fellow contributors, we will first use Simmel's thesis to elucidate the thematic background of our writings.

Simmel argues that money is 'function without substance'; it is a mere instrumental expression of the relationship between subject (the human being) and object (his/her environment). As an instrument, however, money allows subjects to invest 'objects' (products, services and relationships) with abstract value, regardless of their particular, individual qualities. Objects can then be quantitatively exchanged, and hence be made uniform. This is how money, as a transparent and universally intelligible medium, emancipates the subject, as it liberates from natural or social restraints. And in this way, the abstract instrument of money can provide societies with a vigorous energy.

Simmel nevertheless also observed - already at the beginning of the twentieth century - that money was increasingly becoming a 'great disruptor'. Although money is 'simply' a quantitative expression of individual qualitative relationships, there is no indispensable connection between the two, and the instrumental, extrinsic function therefore has the tendency to detach from exactly the intrinsic qualities it expresses. Money in itself inherently tends towards becoming *more* essence (function) and *less* substance. This is already exemplified by the changing appearance of money: from seashells and cattle, via coins and bills, to scriptural money and bitcoins. Simmel argues that in this way, the greatest blessing bestowed on us by modern money – the possibility of exchanging 'things' – also poses the greatest danger to our culture and society. Money only expresses completely interchangeable, anonymous, and functional characteristics, as these *are* its own functions. But by doing so, it hides the concrete reality of 'value', or the *valuable relationship* between subject and object. Money itself obscures the relationship between man and the world.

Paradoxically, next to obscuring our disposition of value, money also symbolizes it. Or, as Simmel states it: 'money is the adequate expression of the relationship of man to the world'. For the more abstract money becomes – and with it, the relationship it expresses between subjective *valuations* and objective *values* – the harder it becomes to concretize value. In modern times, abstract money allows us to value any object by price, but the price of an object will no longer necessarily tell us something about its value. It is therefore the triumph of the amorphous availability of *everything through function* over the individual significance of *anything by substance*, as explicated by our money, that we, modern people, will have to struggle with, according to Simmel.

When considering modern times, it is evident that culture and society have changed drastically over the last forty-odd years. Radical shifts in domains such as technology, economics, (geo)politics, and (social) media have turned the world into a global village. One exponent of these shifts has been the immense growth of the global financial sector. On the one hand, this process of financial globalisation has gone hand in hand with a considerable worldwide net growth of wealth; on the other hand, as the financial crisis of 2007/8 has shown, there are serious and harmful downsides to this global financial interconnectedness. In the wake of the crisis it has become painfully clear how 'real' financial products can turn out to be, (again) proving their 'value'. Anyone who all of a sudden is unable to pay the mortgage instalments will find that finance is not all that abstract.

For obvious reasons, the adverse sides of the globalized financial sector have been the main focus of political action, media coverage and public debate in recent years. Public resentment with the sector was and still is quite large and, at least since 2008, it has been under close scrutiny by the polity. And not without results: things *have* changed since the crisis. Stricter regulation, more substantive external monitoring and higher capital requirements, as well as increased attention for CSR, ethics and culture, to name a few issues. And yet, in the past months and years, there is one question that returns again and again: has anything *really* changed? Have technical, legal, and functional measures done the job? Or are the underlying social dynamics, the culture, and the ethics of the financial sector virtually the same as they were before the crisis? Even more fundamentally, what was the real problem in the financial sector to begin with? Was it a 'technical' problem? Institutional? Individual? Cultural? Or ethical? And did it only affect the financial sector, or was it more widespread – affecting other commercial industries, the government, and society itself?

Paul Dembinski, director of the Swiss *Observatoire de la Finance*, connects Simmel's theory of money to the dynamics in society as exemplified by the rise and fall of the financial sector in the past few decades. He proposes the term 'financialisation': the increased dominance of financial (functional) motives in the domains of economy and society. Or, in his own words: 'the almost total triumph of transactions over relationships'. Following Dembinski's interpretation of Simmel, it is clear how the idea of functional money connects to the process of financialisation. Money as mere function becomes ever more abstract, shapeless – *fluid*. This abstract money brings us comfort and ease, as it is safer and easier to handle (re digital banking), and it affords new financial instruments. But following this same 'functional (financial) logic', abstract money penetrates easily and deeply, and almost irreversibly, into the organization of our societies. Accompanied, and strengthened by, the many other technological, cultural and geopolitical developments of the last decades, money has been able to abstract ever more qualitative values, extending to domains where money was not present hitherto. *That which is fluid flows wherever it can*; a financial logic has seeped into all capillaries of our society. We now see 'our world' through a financial perspective; all has come to stand in the light of money.

Although it is clear that the dynamics in the financial sector are the offspring of a broad societal evolution, it is safe to say that it now also functions as a catalyst, if only for the sector being a prime example of a domain where functionality overrules relationships and the value of concrete social interdependencies has become obscured by an abstract shroud of complexity, as was clearly displayed in the aftermath of the mortgage crisis. Furthermore, the financial sector itself has proved to have (had) a tendency to develop financial instruments that justify and consolidate unbalanced relationships, thereby further stimulating the cultural financialisation.

'What has been seen cannot be unseen' the saying goes. Thus, it is impossible to simply unsee our financialized perspective. We can however strive to elaborate new perspectives. That is why this book pursues *Finance for the Common Good*. We, the editors of this volume, believe that no single discours can account for the co-evolution of finance, economy and society in the last decades, inextricably intertwined as it has been with technical, political, legal, psychological, social and cultural developments. Hence, it makes no sense to demand change only from the financial sector, as some have falsely done. We do, however, believe that the term 'financialisation' gives adequate expression to the direction taken by modern societies in the past four or five decades, and that this is evidently made visible in and around the financial sector. We – society – have made money and with it, the financial sector, too much of a mere 'function'. The result has been a 'finance' that only benefited the 'financial good'.

Fortunately, further financialisation is not inevitable; our degrees of freedom are not (yet) exhausted. As editors, we are convinced that this is especially true for the countries that have strong roots in the rich tradition of the Rhineland model, that of the 'Gemeinschaft', the 'Commons', or the 'Polder'. This is a geographic- and cultural area where relational finance could still be a viable organisational principle. In this volume, we therefore wish to explore the possibilities for a healthy Rhinelandic arrangement vis-à-vis an all-too financialised global village. Our main question in this is: how can the financial sector once again help achieve sustainable relationships and social ties? And under which circumstances, in what kind of environment, can such a change take place? Can we re-actualise the

Rhineland model to enter a new social era, one in which the government, the financial sector, businesses, and society can complement one another and enable human flourishing, a vital society, and a healthy planet?

The initiative for this book was taken by the Socires (*Society & Responsibility*) foundation, an independent think tank engaged with questions at the interface of culture and society. The book reflects the findings of our *Ethics and Finance* programme, which took place between 2015 and 2018. This programme is now continued under the title *Finance and the Common Good*. The various authors who have contributed to this book were all involved in the programme at some stage. They were all invited to share their thoughts in a written contribution on the topic. We are very thankful for their contributions, at our events as well as in this particular volume.

Modesty with regard to the impact of this book is in order. We do not pretend to come up with any kind of solution to the financial sector. There are plenty of solutions already, offered by just as many commentators. We believe that at the moment, there is a need to develop an appreciation for the complexity of the issues at hand. Furthermore, we believe it is necessary to foster willingness in all interested parties to enter into dialogue on these issues. We must come to appreciate that everyone must change in some way or another, to ensure that nothing stays the same. This book is meant as a means to clear some of the way on the journey towards finance for the common good.

The book consists of four parts, which are preceded by an essay by former President of Socires, **Mr. Jos van Gennip**. He will introduce the theme of the book and explain the 'Socires approach', in which he also clarifies why it is that Socires believes it is able to make a sensible contribution to the current debate on the financial sector. Then, in **Part 1, Finance and Financialisation,** five authors will investigate what financialisation is all about and how it impacts the financial sector in relationship to society and the state. Former Dutch Minister of Finance **Wouter Bos** looks back at the financial crisis of 2008 and its aftermath, concluding with a trenchant question: do we really need another crisis to finally learn our lessons? **Professor Dirk Bezemer** describes the socio-economic history of financialisation and the disastrous effects this process has had. He shows us how everything of real value, by financialisation, has actually become, paradoxically, financially less valuable. **Professor Eelke de Jong** continues this line of thought and adds: a truly honest and open dialogue on financialisation is imperative, especially in politics. As political unwillingness to intervene was one of the causes for the previous crisis, politicians should now draw their conclusions and act to prevent another one. Independent advisor **Roland Kupers** connects ideas about financialisation and the financial crisis to systems- and complexity theory. He considers the possibilities such theories offer with regards to restructuring our economic system. He believes it is about time that such a reconstruction of the financial sector takes place. **Professor Govert Buijs** argues that the failure of institutional order – by which he explicitly refers to the financial sector – is at the origin of populism and political unrest. He argues that restoring the 'economic trinity' is the first step towards a revitalisation of relationships within society.

The central question of **Part 2, Finance and Relations**, is whether relationships can be placed at the heart of the financial sector. **Professor Lans Bovenberg** argues that things already go wrong in secondary-level education. If we teach the youth about a world of markets and competition, it should be no surprise that when they reach adulthood, they will interact with the world according to these principles. Prof. Bovenberg suggests that we approach economics and the financial sector from a relational perspective. **Cor van Beuningen and Kees Buitendijk**, of the Socires' Finance and the Common Good program, reflect on the phenomenon of financialisation with relation to culture and society. They also discuss the various excesses of financialisation and the possible ways of inverting negative developments: to move toward Finance for the Common Good. **Professor Johan Graafland** discusses the effects of relational thinking on our economy and on our society, asking whether market and morals, or the economy and relationships, are compatible in the first place. **Christiaan Vos**, philosopher and fiscal-economist, addresses a similar question. He argues that the role of ethics in society is to prevent all kinds of harm, but in finance ethical considerations seems to be no longer key.

To prevent immoral outcomes of business decisions we need to re-enable employees to bring morality to the work floor.

In **Part 3, Relational Finance: Regulation, Policies, Practice**, we discuss the implications of relational finance, with particular focus on the way it would take shape in various domains of finance. **Theodor Kockelkoren**, former member of the board of directors of the Dutch Authority for Financial Markets (AFM), observes a collective obsession with supervision and regulation, which ultimately has the paradoxical effect of undermining morality. He argues for value-driven supervision. **Professor Sylvester Eijffinger** looks back on the work of the Maas Committee back in 2009, asking which changes have (not) taken place in the financial sector as a result of its findings. According to him, solid, experienced professionals with a strong backbone are needed to curb the risk appetite inherent to banking. **Carla Moonen**, former Chair of the Pension Fund for Care and Wellbeing (Pensioenfonds Zorg en Welzijn), reflects on the implications of Finance for the Common Good for large pension funds. She believes it is time for a fundamental reorientation with regard to how pension savings are invested. Director of the Belgian National Bank, and former Minister of Finance and vice-Prime Minister of Belgium, **Steven Vanackere** offers us a broad view on the question of morality in the modern age. He suggests that short-termism is a persistent trait of our culture. Acknowledging that regulation can have many adverse effects, he nevertheless warns for the disastrous effects of a 'regulatory race to the bottom' at the international level.

In **Part 4, Relational Finance in the World of Tomorrow**, we consider the future of finance: what lies ahead? **Maarten Biermans**, responsible for sustainable capital markets at Rabobank, connects the question of ethics to the challenges FinTech poses for the financial sector. His message: we must think about ethical dilemmas of FinTech now, before reality overtakes us. **Haroon Sheikh**, senior researcher at the Dutch Scientific Council for Government Policy (WRR), discusses the future of the financial sector along two lines: geopolitics and FinTech, and asks: are we ready for the considerable changes that are going to occur in these domains? Former President of the European Council Count **Herman Van Rompuy** considers the implications of the financial crisis and the rise of populism for Europe and the European Union. He explains the necessity of a new agenda for the European Union. Finally, former Prime Minister of the Netherlands **Professor Jan Peter Balkenende** considers a number of overarching questions concerning the global economy and society. He reviews the answers that have been given to these questions in the past, as well as those that are currently being developed. Finally, he addresses the long road that lies ahead. **Rens van Tilburg**, director of the Sustainable Finance Lab – Socires' partner organization for a 2019-2021 program (not coincidentally) titled 'Finance and the Common Good' - concludes this volume. He explores the question: why is there need for a Rhinelandic alternative to the current financial constitution? And how do we bring this kind of systemic change about?

In the **concluding remarks** to the book, the authors of this introduction attempt to unite the various strands of thought that are presented in the essays. How can we make the transition from the conclusions drawn in this book towards a productive dialogue, one that can truly contribute to a different *ethics* of the financial sector? Is there any chance of a Rhineland arrangement of relational finance?

Bibliography

Bevers, Ton. 'De Grote Gelijkmaker.' *De Groene Amsterdammer*, 20 Dec. 1995.

Dembinski, Paul, and Christophe Perraz. 'Towards the Break-Up of Money. When Reality – Driven by Information Technology – Overtakes Simmel's Vision.' *Foresight* 2.5 (2000): 483-496.

Dembinski, Paul. 'Finance: Servant or Deceiver? Financialization at the crossroads'. *Palgrave MacMillan*, 2009

Simmel, Georg. 'The Philosophy of Money'. *Reprint ed. New York: McGraw Hill*, 2008.

The Socires Approach - Finance, State, Society

By Jos van Gennip

FIVE YEARS AGO, Socires took the first steps in setting up its programme on ethics and finance. Some wondered why we - with no particular qualifications in this field - would enter an area that demands so much professional knowledge and expertise. We were aware of our short-comings, yet all the same we forced ourselves from the very start to engage in intensive dialogue with academia, the financial industry, civil organisations, and politics.

This 'diamond approach' has proven very fruitful in the many areas where we promote the concept of a 'responsible society' ('society and responsibility' being the meaning of the acronym 'Socires'). The domain of finance was the very place where an open dialogue was missing. Media and parts of public opinion considered the industry a Leviathan of greed. Being 'too big to fail', in combination with systems of subprime mortgages and other questionable financial products, simply meant that the winners took the profits of their own irresponsible and overly risky dealings. Meanwhile, others - clients and society as a whole - received the blows. Scores of books, journal publications, and opinion articles explicated this analysis and emphasised the feeling of injustice. The system seemed not only to encourage irresponsible behaviour, but was also changing characters and personalities.

It is no wonder that the ensuing mistrust and rift between the banking sector and society has led to an outcry for more regulation, stronger restrictions, and a ceiling on bonuses and salaries. A stricter regulatory regime was indeed imposed. This process is still continuing. However, it is doubtful whether this limited reaction will truly allow the system to avoid a new crisis. At the same time, the real risks of overregulation loom.

There is an alternative, ethics-based approach in which bankers and professionals in the finance industry promote awareness for a broad responsibility that surpasses the interest of their own pockets or share-holders of the company. Could this be a viable solution? It would mean a total conversion of the minds of bankers and big players in the finance industry. The financial sector would now assume the role of servant to the real economy, to the wellbeing of clients and their communities, to sustainability, and even to the protection of the earth. Is this a realistic perspective? The newly implemented banker's oath points in this direction. UNIAPAC, the confederation of Christian entrepreneurs, has made strong pleas to frame banking as a 'noble vocation'. However, one of our main advisors, former Minister and top banker Onno Ruding, has expressed doubts as to whether such symbolic gestures are effective. They may certainly contribute to the much needed change of culture, but more is needed. A strong reflection on and a far-reaching awareness of the role and function of the sector and the mentality of the individual banker are required. This must be combined with a strong institutional and collective adherence to high ethical and moral standards and behaviour. Granted, the role and mentality of the individual are indispensable. All the same, change in this regard is only effective in combination with a change of (and binding consequences for) the culture of the individual company.

But even all that will be insufficient if we do not manage to translate the complex causes of the 2008 banking crisis into consequences for all parties involved: the financial sector, the state, and society as a whole (i.e. business, academia, media, and the wider public). Every element in this triangle has to pursue an agenda of reform, and above all engage in a process of open and structural dialogue with the other elements. The central thesis of our discussions in this book is that a realistic perspective for a structural solution must involve all three actors.

The financial industry

The first step in the process is for the financial sector to recognise the need to break with its current mentality. This mentality insists that whatever is not forbidden (or not regulated) is therefore permitted. This attitude has resulted in a notorious range of so-called 'innovative' products, most of which are not understood by clients and are hardly transparent. It was exactly the utilisation of this type of not-forbidden-but-very-hazardous products that caused the downfall and near-collapse of the entire financial system. One of the outcomes of the crisis should be a regular dialogue between banks and external and internal supervisory boards and authorities on how to deal with innovations, new technological opportunities, and this grey area in general. The role of the supervisor should include far more than simply checking the bank's compliance with written regulations.

This goes much further. The financial sector should comply with new provisions for stronger buffers and extended internal risk reduction, but above all it should be more responsive to the real needs and demands of clients, stakeholders, the economy, society, and the earth. This means the sector can no longer perceive itself as an autonomous, self-propelling force that primarily serves its own interests. Is this a utopian vision? We discern hopeful signs of change in the way in which certain banks deal with their clients: they accept a broader responsibility. We also sometimes observe far-reaching change in vision and in investment criteria on the part of certain pension funds and life insurance companies. In their opinion, long-term value creation is fully compatible with promoting the common good of clients, society, the real economy, and ecology. As Carla Moonen, former President of pension fund PZFW, remarks in her contribution: '[Our nurses do not want] large differences to exist between 'lucky' and 'unlucky' generations; [they prefer] solidarity between generations'.

However, there is a strong tendency to return to 'business as usual' now that the worst of the crisis seems to have passed. It seems to have passed, because a new crisis (possibly worse than the previous one) is a very serious risk - and this time our means for repair and containment are nearly exhausted. A number of practices of the nineties and the early years of this millennium are reappearing: exuberance in bonuses and salaries, a sometimes inflated stock market and an ever-expanding financialisation taking place in our economies. Once again, the financial industry cherishes its semi-autonomous status and existence. It is detached from the real economy and from society as a whole.

Society

It is no surprise that society's reaction to a financial crisis will be distrust, alienation, and a search for financial services provided by non-banking institutions. And there is more. Many share the opinion that populist movements in Western democracies have gained momentum because of this distrust and alienation, and because of the perception that the state and politics are unable to carry out a substantial and effective reform of the system. This combination of alienation and distrust, together with concerns about income inequality, loss of traditional jobs, the as yet unpaid societal and individual bills of the previous crisis, globalisation, concerns about illegal migration flows and the erosion of originally strong political parties, could completely destroy the broad post-war consensus of interdependence. It could even damage the value of democracy itself. This could be the ultimate outcome of irresponsible behaviour and a corrupted culture in a single sector of society. We therefore have no other choice than to find sustainable solutions and arrive at new perspectives for the financial industry.

Meanwhile, we have to recognise that society (including academia) had a strong co-responsibility for the last crisis. One of the striking remarks in the Socires seminars was that immediately after the crisis, it was absolutely unheard of to refer to this co-responsibility. The sector alone was to blame. Perhaps politicians were too: they had been unable to control the sector. Meanwhile institutions, social movements, media, and even the university stayed largely silent in the long, structural build-up to the 2008 disaster. When the IMF's chief economic strategist and a top investor at Wall Street predicted the crisis and stressed the unsustainability of the system, their voices were largely ignored. Cognitive bias dominated publicity and favoured ignorance, over-optimism, and risk denial.

It goes even further, both in the US and in Europe. It is our very culture, our very civilisation that fuelled the crisis: a culture of overconsumption and spending, instead of saving and practising sobriety. In the words of a banker, speaking at one of the Socires seminars: the crisis is to blame on the 'loan addiction' of consumers and banks alike - a culture which seems hardly to have been changed by the experiences of the last ten years. Some religious leaders have called it a civilisation of hedonism and hyper-individualism, where fame and merit are defined by the pursuit of wealth and riches.

We cannot isolate a single incident - however severe it might be - from these underlying trends in our civilisation, a 'civilisation of indifference', that caused the 2008 banking crisis and subsequent Eurocrisis. We find a parallel with the ecological crisis, where individuals feel alienated from the natural environment. At the height of the crisis, Deputy Prime Minister of the Netherlands, Wouter Bos, was asked who was to blame for it. His stunning answer: 'All of us!' He hardly received recognition for this analysis, but he was right.

The state and politics

The state and politics should continue to develop a legal and institutional framework that fosters less risk for both clients and the system itself. This framework requires a better balance between rewards and punishment. The state and politics should also enable supervisory authorities to assume tasks that exceed mere compliance with existing regulations: they should be able to address the role of banks and financial institutions in promoting the social and common good. At the same time, politicians must become aware that rule-stacking in an effort to tame a single actor - the financial sector - is neither effective nor fruitful. Overregulation will hamper the entrepreneurial space required by the industry to take the lead in achieving effective reforms. It must be recognised that the financial sector is indispensable for a flourishing economy and the wellbeing of citizens.

In certain situations, we require self-restraint of the state. In others, we need the state to develop and implement new policies. The latter is particularly needed in situations where the state and politics bear a strong co-responsibility for 'debt addiction' in society and the state apparatus itself. How sustainable are policies that favour borrowing and punish saving? Politicians should question the consequences of their own appetite for borrowing and debt. They should also consider what might happen to a society that favours overbuying and overconsumption, notably with borrowed resources. What are the limits to the debt burden and to society's capacity to earn back its expenses? What is the fall-out of the current artificially low interest rates and the ensuing, irresistible temptation of borrowing ever more money? What are the implications of the debt burden when it comes to aging populations, incidentally shrinking economies, and the competition between necessary collective public investments and individual consumption? And how do we finance the enormous cost of climate and environmental investments? Finally, how do we include in our spending behaviour the true cost to the environment? Perhaps this is where the central challenge for our democracy lies: at the point where long-term responsible measures appear to be completely at odds with electoral short-term gains. Who has the courage to address these new challenges, even if it means losing the next election? It is urgent that new policies are accepted that encourage saving and frugality; policies that replace the current ones stimulating spending and borrowing.

People

The fourth actor is the main element in the reform of the system: the individual. Although it is imperative to have an environment that enables personal changes in behaviour and attitudes, nothing will change without a personal will to reset. This is where ethics and moral convictions come in. This is the domain of education, of convictions, of culture and civilisation, and of one's own personality. There are limited possibilities of outside interference in this regard. But some do exist. One of the contributors to the Socires programme works intensively on a reform of our secondary-level economics education. Others plea for the introduction of a moral and ethical dimension in management schools. We follow with admiration the growing interest at the academic and even the students' level for other considerations than fast profits. Socires contributes regularly to conferences, studies, and policy recommendations in which the relationship between the economy and the common good is made central. It is not helpful to only preach and blame. There is a growing awareness among new generations that certain parts of the current system have no future, because they have destructive consequences. This is a basis on which we can build. Young people's desire to achieve a financial industry that serves the real economy, the well-being of society, and the Earth is even more promising. Particularly the reforms that are taking place in the pension and insurance sectors can have positive consequences for professionals' job satisfaction and meaning of life.

Unfortunately, individuals in this case often have to function in an environment that is not very conducive to changes in attitude. Take for instance the developments in ICT, which foster more anonymity and detachment rather than the much-needed restoration of the personal relationship between banker and client. Meanwhile, the banker has to function in a cultural climate that is hardly conducive to the promotion of stakeholders' interests and the common good. It is our shared responsibility as clients and as general public to applaud and endorse company policies which put long-term value creation above short-term profits, prudence above high risks, and precautionary principles above passing the bill to the next generation.

And there is more. What importance do job satisfaction and responsible, future-oriented behaviour have in a culture that prefers ranking high in terms of income and wealth, as well as exhibiting purchasing power and luxury spending? Again, the discussion on the reform of the financial system and its relevance and long-term security meets the sphere of culture and civilisation.

Next steps

In recent years we are fortunate to have observed an increasing sensitivity for this cultural and social dimension. In the Earth Charter, in the Papal Encyclical Laudato Si, at Davos, and in initiatives such as the Global Compacts and especially the Sustainable Development Goals (SDGs), we sense the need for a broader approach. Against this background, this study can only be a modest contribution to a very complex issue. But it is an essential contribution. We are convinced that this triangular dialogue is the only way to achieving a comprehensive perspective for necessary corrections and maybe even alternative arrangements in the financial sector.

During these past five years, in which we engaged critically with the topic at hand and joined discussions and studies, we came to a second conclusion. We even discovered a new frontier. For more than forty years, society, politics, and the economy have been tempted towards a specific interpretation of the market economy: the Anglo-Saxon interpretation. Some have referred to this type of market-dominated economy as 'casino-capitalism', others as 'capitalisme sauvage'. This model stands in contrast to a different interpretation of the market economy, namely the Rhineland or social market model. The latter model has been characteristic to the reconstruction of a number of economies in Western Europe. There is no doubt that both systems have certain advantages, at the very least for some segments of the population. However, in the Rhineland model, the costs of the welfare state, certain forms of overprotection in the labour market, governmental regulations, and state interference became unbearable or caused considerable friction. Meanwhile, the Anglo-Saxon model could not contain its inherent excesses and its sometimes destructive consequences.

A logical question came up during our deliberations. Is there a system that can integrate the demands of the economy, society, ecology, and the stunning developments that have recently taken place in other areas? Globalisation demands more flexibility; digitalisation and robotisation demand a different organisation of the labour market; demographic developments require a different pension and life insurance system; and FinTech can affect dominant positions of the banking system with its unforeseen support for freeriding. FinTech also constitutes a serious challenge to the regulatory system that was developed in the wake of the 2008 crisis. For all of us concerned with the survival of the financial system and its relevance for the 'real' economy, it is indispensable to engage with the actualisation, or even the reinvention, of the Rhineland model. It is about time that those actors who deal with contemporary challenges in the financial sector also engage in this project of the future. A global, technologically updated and ecologically relevant system should be on the agenda for new studies, conferences, and programmes.

Our January 2018 conference ended with a plea to embed the financial discussion in the broader discussion on the reinvention of the Rhineland model. It also made a proposal to further internationalise the debate. Can we work to achieve consensus among a number of like-minded

European countries, mostly members of the Eurozone and geographically located (in the broadest sense) around the Rhine? First of all, this is necessary because our interdependence makes separate national reforms of the financial or even the economic system futile and obsolete. Even more importantly, the necessary global and multilateral dimensions of these reforms demand a coordinated policy by a bloc of like-minded countries. This bloc must be as strong and as influential as possible. Is this wishful thinking? A paradoxical development is taking place today, where voters and leaders from the erstwhile pillars of the multilateral Anglo-Saxon system (the US and UK) are now distancing themselves from it. Some even seek to undermine and destroy it. This even applies to those who up to now were most reluctant to critically evaluate the Anglo-Saxon system. They admit that new alliances should take shape as soon as possible, along with a new architecture of the international financial system. This is because the international financial system plays an important role in defending multilateral mechanisms and forms of regulation and protection of the globalisation process for a considerable part of the world population.

A timely reflection

This publication comes at a strategic moment for the interconnected approach. A lot is at stake in the year 2019: the dependability of the system, the redefinition of a European model of economics, and the strength of multilateral and global financial and economic structures.

The Netherlands is the seat of a number of very important global financial players. It is key that a discussion on financialisation takes place in the country. However, the wounds of the crisis may have been too fresh five years ago. An objective and detached discussion about causes and responsibilities was not yet possible. In Europe, we were engaged in a struggle to save the Euro. At the multilateral level, there was a - misplaced - optimism about global cooperation and agreements. Today, the dependability of our national financial system is once again taken for granted. This is partly caused by what might well be the lowest interest rates in history. The worst of the Eurocrisis seems to have come and gone, which can be attributed at least in part to the leadership and guidance of a number of contributors to our programme: Herman Van Rompuy, Jan Peter Balkenende, and Wouter Bos. However, at the global level confusion and frustration prevail. New leadership and vision is needed. One thing is clear: we must utilise the current years to the utmost in order to achieve a structural reform of our own financial system and to consolidate the improvements that were made post-2008. Europe will receive a new Commission and a new Parliament in 2019, and it faces the task of bridging between the rescue phase and the phase in which a future-proof regime is achieved. Worldwide, we must develop a vision and build alliances that allow us to avert a collapse of the global cooperation structure. On top of all this, we must learn to handle the revolutionary developments and breakthroughs of technological innovations, which are shaking the traditional banking system to its very foundations as we speak.

At stake are the health and proliferation of our financial system, the relationship between an inclusive economy and the common good, and the survival of a financial world order of equity and justice.

PART 1

Finance and Financialisation

Looking Back at the Banking Crisis: Did We Learn Anything?[1]

By Wouter Bos

ON 22 FEBRUARY 2010, I closed the doors behind me at the Ministry of Finance in The Hague. My job was done. I had spent three years dealing with banks and collapsing (or nearly collapsing) economies. This was not exactly what I had anticipated when I first became Minister of Finance.

What happened in 2008?

Perhaps the easiest way to illustrate our surprise at the turn of events in 2008 is by explaining how we dealt with the budget for the year 2009. Drafting the budget is a process that starts in spring. The idea is that one only needs to apply a finishing touch to the budget during the summer period. Then, the new budget is presented on Prinsjesdag ('Prince Day'), the third Tuesday of September. Of course, this is done by a very proud Minister of Finance.

We did indeed prepare the budget. We wrote beautiful paragraphs about the year to come. This was supposed to be an extremely successful year in terms of the economy. We were going to reduce the national deficit and our debt.

Let me tell you two anecdotes that explain what really happened. I presented the budget on Tuesday, 16 September 2008. The text was sent to the editor and printer about ten days earlier. Four days before I presented the budget in parliament, I presented it - under embargo - to the national press. Then, one day before I put on my dress suit and sealed the budget in the usual golden briefcase, the Lehman Brothers Bank fell. The next day I stood in parliament with an outdated budget, in a world that had changed overnight.

Obviously, we were not able to reduce the national deficit and debt in the wake of the start of the banking crisis. On the contrary; I believe I now top the list of Dutch Ministers of Finance that have raised the public debt at breakneck speed.

All of this happened in 2008. Hectic years followed. With every decision we took on whether to support a failing bank or not, we knew a lot was at stake. But what exactly was at stake? We did not know. Neither did we know what exactly we should do. What we experienced had never happened before. There were no works of reference available to me - nothing that told me what to do. Only as the crisis developed did we learn what exactly was happening, and what had caused it to happen. At a global level, we spoke about imbalances in the world economy. At a system level, we spoke about regulation and incentives. At the level of behaviour, we spoke about bankers and bonuses. But at the most fundamental level, we spoke about ourselves.

On 8 December 2008 I was a guest on a popular Dutch talk show called 'De Wereld Draait Door' ('As the World Turns'). The presenter, Matthijs van Nieuwkerk, asked me who was to blame for the crisis. I was fairly sick and tired of blaming bankers once again... And so I said it was us.

He looked at me and asked 'Us?'. And I said: 'Yes. We want high pensions, we want high returns on our savings and we want consumption against low prices, so in the end we want the financial sector to misbehave because we ask for high returns and what they come with: high risks'.

In all of my twelve years in politics, this was probably one of the moments that I was criticized most by the general public. The number of critical responses in newspapers and on websites, blogs, and other media, was huge. How did I dare blame us, noble citizens, instead of the bankers?

It's all about us

Robert Reich wrote beautiful books about this phenomenon. He teaches us we all carry more than one soul in our chest. Goethe's description of 'zwei Seelen im Brust' ('Two souls, alas, are housed within my breast') is way too simple if you want to describe how inconsistent we are in our behaviours. Reich tells us that we are citizens, as well as consumers, investors, and money savers. And we are all of those at the same time.

However, our goals and intentions are different in each of these roles. The citizen in us wants democracy, human rights, and decent labour conditions. The consumer wants low prices and cheap imports. The investor wants high returns. The pension saver wants a safe and high pension. And then Reich tells us what really happens: the citizen in us always loses. In the end, the soul that argues for morality loses from other souls arguing for returns, profits, and low prices. My favourite example in this regard has to do with trade unions in the Netherlands. For years, they governed investment funds that were charged with the responsibility to invest for pension funds. As trade unions, they opposed the high bonuses and risk-taking prevalent in the financial sector. As administrators for pension funds, trying to maximise benefits for their members, they were responsible for paying out those same bonuses to the boards of the investment funds.

I am not sure whether this explanation would have landed well on that TV show and whether it would have made my response any more popular. Probably not. All the same, this is one of the lessons I learned from the crisis: the causes of it go deep into the veins of our society, our economic behaviours and our morality. The latter pertains not only to the morality of bankers, but at least as much to the morality of us, citizens, in our various roles of consumers, investors, and money savers.

Can we change?

The question at hand is the following. Is it worth it to study this conviction, in the hope of avoiding a next crisis - meanwhile, of course, improving the relationship between the state, the financial sector, and society? Let me elaborate on that in two ways. First of all, this is going to be extremely difficult. We may, in fact, need another crisis to solve it. It would not be the first time that we need a crisis to truly change our behaviour.

Some of the most breath-taking experiences I had while in politics, at least to me personally, were the various G20-conferences I attended during the peak of the banking crisis. I witnessed issues being discussed that were never discussed; I saw countries work together who never worked together; I saw new regulations being discussed that before were never even permitted on the agenda; I saw policies being considered that aimed at de-globalising financial markets. The latter took place while only months before the crisis, we all believed in the gospel of globalising markets, and were convinced that globalisation was unstoppable and irreversible.

It lasted six, perhaps twelve months. And then it was over. The crisis was over. And very soon, the incredible G20-discussion, that at times had looked and felt like a world government at work, quickly became shallow and lost their ambition and power. We had in no way completed our policy agenda. The financial sector was rescued, and so the urgency left the system and more and more of the players went back to business as usual.

Can we change the system? Can we change the triangle of Finance, State, and Society, without a good crisis? I honestly do not know. Certainly, national politics have manoeuvred themselves into very difficult positions. They are now hardly able to change market dynamics that are fundamentally international.

The Turkish-American economist Dani Rodrik, of whom I am a big fan, is one of the most interesting economists writing about these dilemmas today. He describes his own triangle, which he calls the 'trilemma of globalisation' (Rodrik 2012).

Rodrik argues that we are trying to reconcile three goals that cannot be reconciled. First of all, we want national sovereignty; second, we want democracy; and finally, we want to benefit from international trade. He argues that there is always a trade-off: you cannot have it all.

In posing his trilemma, Rodrik shows us a peculiar perspective on the rise of populism. Traditional mainstream politicians like to blame populists for making promises they cannot keep. Yet Rodrik demonstrates that mainstream politicians make promises they cannot keep either, by promising maximal benefits from international trade *and* democracy *and* sovereignty. Populists are actually more honest in this regard, by claiming that either national sovereignty or democracy is being sacrificed by promoting globalised trade.

Rodrik describes the Bretton Woods arrangements as a choice for national sovereignty and democracy over globalising trade (2012: 69-83). The Washington consensus, in his analysis, represents the choice for national sovereignty and globalisation over democracy. And should we ever choose a world government, it would mean the choice for democracy and globalisation and democracy over national sovereignty. Rodrik's point is that we can get two out of three options, but never all three.

He also raises the interesting question of whether we still have a choice as to which two out of three options we would like to choose. Rodrik observes the dominant position held by promoters of globalising trade, and argues that this will always come at the expense of either national sovereignty or democracy. He is not always consistent himself, but seems to choose national sovereignty and democracy over the promotion of global trade. In his latest books, he tries to convince the reader that if we can globalise markets, we can also de-globalise them and revive national sovereignty and democracy.

The reason I mention Rodrik here is that I applaud his analysis and his idealism. Whatever has been globalised can also be de-globalised!

Or can it?

There are two possible problems here. The first of these is that globalisation is far easier than de-globalisation. National politics has created international and multinational players by removing borders and globalising markets. Politicians have created forces that are stronger than they are and it is often hard to see who controls whom.

The second problem follows from the first. If politics remains national and the key players remain international and are subject to international market dynamics, politicians will always lose. This is because international businesses, whether financial or of some other kind, will always be able to evade national restrictions on their market behaviour. This can only be avoided if politics and policy-making start taking place at an international level. However, that would mean sacrificing a significant amount of national sovereignty or national democracy.

Let us put it differently. Rodrik is right to say that aiming for ever more globalisation comes at the expense of national sovereignty and/or democracy. The problem, however, is that this probably also holds for the process of de-globalisation.

Rationally speaking, the best way forward would be through some form of global or European governance. This would indeed be at the expense of national sovereignty and national democracy. It is a way forward – but a very fragile one at that.

In a political sense, I consider myself a child of the year 2005. This was the year in which we put the so-called European Constitution to the people of Europe by means of a referendum. Two-thirds of the electorate voted to reject the constitution. Politicians across the political spectrum all reacted the same way. 'Be more careful with the European project', they thought – 'if not, we risk losing even more public support'. This meant slowing down integration; slowing down expansion; and above all, never crossing the line.

Somehow, something else entirely happened. In reaction to the financial crisis of 2008, European governments coordinated policies like never before, and transferred considerable amounts of power to the Union. I believe this was the right choice – nevertheless, it was completely contrary to the conclusion many politicians drew from the outcome of the referendum in 2005. And perhaps public support did not make that same radical turn.

Rationally, the right thing to do might be to take another step forward in terms of European integration. This would be yet another step away from national sovereignty. However, this will increase the fragility of public support for the European project – and perhaps push it past breaking point. One would almost conclude that an easier way forward would be to create another crisis. But that is of course a route I would not dare recommend…

1. This essay is an adaptation of the keynote lecture by Wouter Bos at Socires Conference 'The Finance-State-Society Triangle in Europe', which took place on 23 January 2018 at Vrije Universiteit, Amsterdam.

Bibliography

Rodrik, Dani. *The Globalisation Paradox*. Oxford: University Press, 2012.

Financialisation: on Price, Value, Rules and Behaviour

By Dirk Bezemer

Introduction

IN THIS ESSAY, I will discuss two dimensions of financialisation. First of all, I will discuss the difference between adding real value and inflating the price of capital products. Classical economists developed a vocabulary for this practice that we seem to have forgotten. Central to this vocabulary is the difference between investment and speculation, as well as the question of what may be considered productive.

A second dimension of financialisation is the idea that our behaviours are purely based on financial deliberations. This idea has permeated our society and suppresses other motivations that are imperative to retaining cohesion in society. Furthermore, it has led to the use of numerical targets as a measure for our performance – as well as the accompanying machinery of administration and measurement tools to continuously assess whether we are meeting these targets. I will draw upon an early 16th-century Dutch text, the *Mariken van Nimwegen*, to argue that such rules impede the 'art' of our work.

By and large this is hardly a positive enumeration. And indeed, it is hard to perceive anything positive when it comes to financialisation. We understand financialisation as the application of the logic of finance to domains where it does not belong: where cost/benefit analyses, the tracking of virtual and fluctuating wealth, or the use of financial stimuli are harmful rather than beneficial. For this reason, we must consider the ubiquity of 'the financial', which we have come to understand in the concept of 'financialisation'. We must do this to better identify the domains where the financial aspect should remain subordinate, even if this goes against our own customs. We must also do this to better understand which elements of our society require protection against our drive to quantify, settle and optimise. This essay strives to be a starting point for this process.

Everything of value?

Our economy is marked by a dividing line, though we are not usually aware of this. I am referring to the difference between value increase (inflating the price of capital products) and value creation (adding value in the economic process), such as the added value which is taxed by VAT. As with all things that matter, this difference is hard to identify conclusively. Yet when the difference is seen in operation, it is easy to suspect that something strange is taking place.

The difference between increase and creation is based in the difference between value and price – a distinction which has spawned numerous studies, yet remains completely foreign to students because it has not been mentioned in lecture halls for over thirty years. It also concerns the difference between speculation and investment and between productive and non-productive activity – yet another concept that is unfamiliar to contemporary economics. National accounts (such as those by the Dutch Bureau of Statistics) operate on the principle that every payment is balanced by a service provided or a ware acquired. Why else did this payment take place? To make this account work, creative tricks are needed – a home, for instance, is considered to provide 'living services'. In this way, the expenses associated with home ownership can be attributed to the living services I have received. This is of course very consistent… But something does not add up.

Classical economists approached this problem in a different way. Aside from income (such as profit or wages), they perceived the so-called *rents*. These *rents* are the 'rewards' that originate solely from property. The landowner whose land increases in value because of the construction of a road across it will acquire the added value in *rents* – not as income. He did not have to take any action. *Rents*, according to classical economists, are not the result of production – the way profit and wages are – but should be deducted from profit and wages. This is because they are *rewards* for production. The 'renter' does not add anything; he skims. He acquires money solely because of his property claim, not because he has contributed to any production process.

The above distinction is often hard to make, but not insurmountable.

Moreover, it is worthwhile to make this distinction: the benefits can be considerable. If *rents* are not essential to any creation of value, they can be taxed away without any damage occurring. Wages and profits, which are after all the impetus to production, will remain untouched. The rents are now no longer skimmed by the renter, but by the state. Value-added tax is harmful to production, income and job security. Value-increased tax is not. We must move from VAT to VIT.

I imagine an advertisement for the Tax Department: 'Wanted: Creative thinkers capable of perceiving the dividing line across sectors and institutions'. Because we are not concerned with eighteenth-century land ownership; we are concerned with the present day. Take the following example. A company uses its profits to buy back its own shares and boost the share price to the advantage of shareholders and to give bonuses to its managers. This is the increase of value, not the creation of it. Did you know that the New York Stock Exchange has not been a place for companies to acquire money for decades? Rather, it is a place where companies can lose their profits in exchange for higher share prices. The stock exchange has become an instrument to convert profits to *rents*. Skimming has become common-place. Or, closer to home: do we truly believe that the average Dutch home, quadrupling in value between 1990 and 2008, now also delivers four times the number of 'living services' to its owner? Of course not. The surge in price was not an indispensable investment in the 'production of living services'. It was mostly the result of generous mortgage approvals that, as we now know, have driven house prices ever higher. Meanwhile, the higher lending rates that are necessary to acquire the house are (usually) deducted from our wages. To state it plainly: banks issued (and households wished for) non-productive loans.

Again and again, the issue at heart is that organisations that should be creating value are devoting themselves to increasing value. If this practice is taxed away, the State will not only acquire money – more importantly, harmful behaviour is deterred.

To invest or to invest

An excellent example of such harmful behaviour is what Milton Keynes dubbed the 'functionless investor'. The idea behind this term was that not all investment is productive. As I write this article, home prices are surging to new heights. The Netherlands are not unique in this regard: in 2017 alone, global real estate investments equalled 1.4 trillion dollars. The Global House Price Index, compiled by the IMF, is at the same level as it was in 2008. 'Time to worry again?', IMF economists recently blogged (Ahir and Loungani 2016). The question answers itself. Bond markets and stock markets are doing well too. Throughout 2017, the Dow Jones has broken record after record.

These markets have one thing in common: they generate immense profits for the owners of real estate, shares and bonds, without requiring any effort on their part. The Dutch are growing fat on the back of their widespread home ownership and mass participation on the bond and stock markets, through their pension funds. Or at least: they profit on average, because economic inequality has seen a strong increase in the Netherlands. How can we explain this?

I recall a 2006 essay bundle compiled of interviews with prominent Dutch academics. One of these academics was economist Lans Bovenberg. He discussed the 'dying rentier economy' problem of the Netherlands. Too often we behave like rentiers, concerned with retaining property above all else; and too seldom do we behave like entrepreneurs, valuing innovation and production above all else. Along with those who manage our financial means, that is to say banks and pension fund managers, we must abandon our search for 'safe' financial returns and instead look for that which truly adds value. They (and we) must behave less like rentiers and more like entrepreneurs, according to Bovenberg in 2006. The date of publication is remarkable – American house prices had just started to decline, and only a year later the financial crisis hit. Bovenberg was well in tune with the times. Precisely the chase of profits from the supposedly extremely safe mortgage derivatives caused the financial crisis. Our pension funds and banks were most heavily invested. Paradoxically so, our desire for safety carried the greatest risks.

But was Bovenberg also correct when he spoke of a 'dying rentier economy'? His choice of words recalls Keynes' famous statement in the last pages of his *General Theory*. Keynes was looking forward to the 'euthanasia of the rentier'; which as mentioned was also referred to by him as the 'functionless investor'. Keynes affiliated himself with the classical school in the economy, which divides all types of income into three groups: profit, wages, and *rent*. Profit and wages are the respective rewards for the use of capital and labour. *Rent* is not a reward for anything: it is allocated to the owner of land, property or financial documents simply by virtue of ownership.

This is what John Stuart Mill called 'the unearned increment': the increase of value, the capital gain that requires no effort whatsoever. Meanwhile it is the effort of entrepreneurs, labourers and the government that makes capital gain possible in the first place. For instance, the government constructs a tram line, causing home owners in the area to reap the profits. Or the ECB injects liquidity into the financial system, causing bond rates to fall, which in turn allows multinationals to obtain cheap financing.

There are three drawbacks. The government pays the costs, does not receive the lion's share of benefits of the tram line, or of *quantitative easing*. The question is for how long the government will be able to keep financing such public works. *Rentier*-wealth also increases the inequality between the haves and have-nots, according to the so-called Matthew-effect: only those who already own assets will grow richer. Furthermore, it becomes harder for newcomers to participate in the process. A young family is now unable to buy a home; the start-up without access to free ECB-money cannot sustain competition with a large company. This is not good for the dynamic of the economy.

No wonder Keynes (in 1936) and Bovenberg (in 2006) wish the rentier a gentle death. It is surprising that both, in their respective era, believed this was about to happen. Alas, this is wishful thinking. Without the existence of active policy in this regard, rentiers will stay alive. They are still among us. In fact – we are rentiers ourselves, if we own a home or contribute to a pension fund. The problem is not the *rentiers* themselves, but rather the policy that *makes* us rentiers.

Thanks to classical economists, this diagnosis is fairly straightforward. So is the solution to the problem: abolishing subsidy on debts and instituting progressive taxes on income and capital. This will mean that labour and entrepreneurship are encouraged, while the chase of capital gains is deterred. Keynes suggests exactly that on the last pages of his *General Theory*. Pay attention, Rutte III! This is not complicated, though it is politically hard to achieve. It is also dearly needed.

Are we productive?

If such a policy is to succeed, we must be clear on what we mean by the dictum 'not all investment is productive'. What is productivity? Say a labourer used to produce twenty tables per day, but now manages thirty: his output per unit of input, and as such his labour productivity, has increased by fifty percent. This is not a new concept: Adam Smith already discussed it. But what kind of output are we talking about here? Is everything that is made or on offer the result of productive processes?

Adam Smith was clear on this: only those who produce goods are productive. Priests, judges, and servants are not. This also applies to shoe shiners, consultants, even insurers and bankers. We clearly enjoy their services, since they make good money, but all the same; they do not produce anything themselves. They can only make a living because others are productive enough to provide for their food, clothing, and other needs. This is what the classical economists would say.

Contemporary, neoclassical economists have slightly extended the idea of productivity. If something is thought of or made and then sold, it has been produced. If more can be produced using the same level of input, productivity has clearly gone up. This approach can lead to peculiar conclusions. I recently attended a lecture discussing the considerable rise of productivity in banks up to 2007. Productivity was measured in terms of loans (output) divided by the hours worked by bank employees (input). If the first skyrockets while the second remains stable, neoclassical economists will drily conclude that productivity is on the rise. End of story. That the issue at stake is a mountain of debt rather than an increase in productivity is a different story. It does not fit the neoclassical discourse of productivity and has therefore been forgotten. If a question is raised concerning this issue, it is denied. This is the power of rhetoric: if the concept is foreign to us, it does not exist.

Casting aside the tidy ecosphere of the neoclassical economist – that is to say, returning to the real world - the problem persists. Does growth in the financial sector add value, and as such, does it result in a greater GDP? Or rather: what would be the size of our economy if we discount the unreliable bankers' GDP (and that of others in the financial services industry)? Jacob Assa, statistician at the UN Headquarters in New York, made a guess. He constructed a new, 'real' GDP, which did not include the questionable contribution of the 'FIRE' (*finance, insurance and real estate*) sector. Hold on tight. Discounting the financial sector, the Dutch economy would be seven percent smaller than it currently is – take away the real estate sector as well and we lose fourteen percent. The British, American, Irish and Australian economies are reduced by a similar amount. Switzerland is decimated. Luxembourg loses a quarter of its GDP. Most other developed economies would be reduced by about three to four percent. These are interesting facts – and they are incredibly useful. For now, however, we must ask the following: did this 'real' GDP grow or shrink under the influence of financial expansion in the past decades?

Assa will have to endure a lot of criticism. This is good. It means that important questions will once again be asked. Is it not rather arbitrary to only discount financial services? What about the others? (But then why consider *all* those services productive?) Are bankers and insurers not fairly useful? (But then why pretend *everything* they do is useful?) And so on and so forth. These investigations will benefit the economy.

Hard incentives and soft norms

The questions that have been asked thus far are all the more urgent because our economy is characterised by the omnipresence of the financial sector. This is evident, for example, from the WRR report *Finance and Society: Restoring the Balance* that was published in 2016.[2] Money is everywhere. Or rather: financially influenced decisions are everywhere. At the core of the problem is our desire to see this dimension of financialisation as the solution rather than the problem. Financial incentives as a miracle cure - sound familiar?

In a financialised environment the financial motive dominates other motives. Examples abound: a housing corporation was established to provide widely accessible, high-quality housing, but its directors are more concerned with investments in derivatives. Choosing a university programme should be based on further developing existing talents, but is often decided by projected graduate incomes which may help pay off debts. The purchase of a house should be about high-quality living, but is more often determined by the amount of mortgage offered. A company exists to create meaningful labour and to produce, but management is more concerned with stock prices. A merger should create synergy between companies, but is in the first place decided by the solvency of the new company and the reward for the managers and their investment banker.

For these reasons, the WRR concludes the following: 'The financial system has become determinant rather than pursuant or facilitating.' What does this mean in daily practice? When we speak of financial systems, we do not only refer to the banking system; there is also an associated system of conduct. What happens if *that* system becomes determinant? Our most important norm would be self-interest. Today, we can hardly imagine the uproar caused by Gordon Gekko's exclamation in 1987: 'Greed is good'. To us he is merely stating the obvious. Greed has become a virtue – only we refer to it as a 'financial incentive'.

Financial incentives might not have become a problem if they produced the desired result without any side effects – the way properly functioning medications do. Unfortunately, this is not the case. A famous experiment in this regard is that of a Haifa day-care, featured in Uri Gneezy and Aldo Rustichini's significantly titled article 'A Fine is a Price' (2000). In an effort to persuade parents to collect their children on time, day-care management imposed a fine on late collections. The desired effect was not achieved – in fact, the opposite happened. More parents started to collect their children late. The researchers explain this phenomenon based on the disappearance of the soft norm. Up to the point where fines were introduced, there was an implicit agreement that children should be collected on time; it was, in a way, a moral obligation to do so. The fines were understood as a signal that late collection was acceptable, as long as the inconvenience was paid for. The hard rule of the financial incentive had replaced the soft norm. A salient detail: the situation proved to be irreversible. Even though the fines were eventually lifted, more parents continued to collect their children late than had been the case before the fines were imposed. The soft moral norm was gone forever. After all, is a fine not simply another price to pay?

Soft norms and intrinsic motivation are the glue of our society. Financialisation undermines this glue and that is a major problem. Time and again, the soft norm of intrinsic motivation is superseded by a hard financial norm. This leads to behavioural problems. Money allows us to compare apples and oranges and it is exactly that practice which facilitates the imposing of financial norms. If a hospital makes less profit than a car dealership, something must be wrong with the hospital. Financial norms and other quantitative measures and targets also lead to futile behaviours – nurses counting their steps, scientists tallying their citations, and schools that *must* be on the top of the list. All in all, we pay a very high price for these supposed advantages.

We are starting to understand this problem. This leads to the following question: how do we get rid of these practices? Financial incentives can be introduced overnight; soft norms cannot. Obtaining trust and having autonomy are preconditions for intrinsic motivation. The shared motivation then becomes a soft norm. That is correct: it all begins with trust. Unfortunately, decades under the reign of neoliberalism have fostered a culture of distrust. One of the results of this has been the proliferation of rules.

Art and rules

The *Mariken van Nimwegen* includes a poem with the central line 'It is the artless who have left art so forlorn'.[3] It is a cry for help from the early sixteenth century that seems eerily contemporary. The *Mariken* speaks of the 'seven liberal arts: rhetoric, music, logic, grammar and geometry, arithmetic and alchemy'.[4] Five centuries later, I would like to expand the list by adding high-quality education, research, healthcare, and more. The *Mariken* states that whomsoever does not understand the art of these can only cause damage. And thus we find that the issue at stake is an old and unfortunately very persistent one. The rise, in many organisations, of a management layer that is unfamiliar with the work of an organisation but does set its rules and financial targets is one of the more detrimental results of financialisation. Let us consider a few examples from the healthcare industry.

A GP reports that he is required to complete five A4 pages of text to obtain dietary food for a terminal patient. Similarly, the requirement of minute-to-minute accountability for care at home ('past the front door') has become infamous. How should one record the time spent walking from the front door of an apartment block to its tenth floor? Where does one 'pass' the front door? And what about a consultation with the patient's GP in their office (not 'past the front door')? The rules of the artless impede the art of good healthcare.

The worst part is that rules seem to proliferate where they are most harmful. Why is this? I would explain this by what I call the 'Mariken Law' – a term I base on the previous dictum from the *Mariken van Nimwegen*. The law is based on the concept of *tacit knowledge*, an idea introduced by Michael Polanyi. *Tacit knowledge* is the knowledge and experience that cannot be recorded in a manual; knowledge that cannot be transferred between people in a matter of hours of classroom instruction. Stocking shelves, peeling bulbs, and the planting of tree cuttings require zero prior experience. One can start immediately. The work of teachers, scientists and carers is completely different – and of course, there are many more professions like theirs.

For what constitutes a good teacher, carer, or researcher? That is hard to say – and unfortunately, this leaves a lot of room for rules to specify these qualifications. (Would you say such rules exist for weeding or stocking shelves? Hardly. It is immediately clear whether the job was done correctly or not.) Meanwhile, rules are most harmful in workplaces that require substantial experience. This is because far too often, rules set by unwitting outsiders force skilled staff to assess and carry out their own work based on misguided benchmarks. This costs a lot of time. Examples abound: devising rankings, counting steps and minutes, ticking boxes in endless charts – I speak from experience. Most of this is a waste of time and hardly an art. This is one half of the Mariken Law. But there is more.

Who do you think suffers most from these practices? Exactly – the artful. Those who pursued a career in education because of the students; who became scientists because they were curious about the world; who work in healthcare because they care. These people are the first to become discouraged. Here we find the other half of the Mariken Law. Rules do not only proliferate in those areas that require expert knowledge and skilled staff; they also force dedicated people out of the field. This is not a coincidence. Accumulating knowledge and acquiring skill require intrinsic motivation. Whoever is intrinsically motivated will find satisfaction in their work, provided it is done well. This means that if the work has to be done in a different way – based on ill-considered rules and benchmarks - they quickly become unmotivated. They cannot bear to change their lesson plan *again* to meet national examination standards; to check the compensation criteria of the insurance company *once more*; or to multiply their number of publications with the H-index of a scientific journal. They will exit the field and find new challenges.

We must not worry about the others – those who do their job to make a living. They will be fine. But let us be honest: they are the 'artless'. If they get to make the rules – and, in good faith, expand them, 'optimise' them, translate them to 'targets' – we will be in a bad place. That is when art is lost, according to the Mariken Law.

1. This essay is based on my columns in *De Groene Amsterdammer* on 15 July 2015, 25 November 2015, 12 October 2016, 28 June 2017, and 2 August 2017.

2. The WRR is the Dutch Scientific Advisory Board for Government Policy. The original title of the report is 'Samenleving en Financiële Sector in Evenwicht'. See also the bibliography.

3. Original: 'Door d'onkonstige gaat die konste verloren.'

4. Original: 'Seven vrie consten: rhetorijcke, musijcke, logica, gramatica ende geometrie, aristmatica ende alkenie.'

Bibliography

Ahir, Hites, and Prakash Loungani. 'Global House Prices: Time to Worry Again?' *IMFBlog*. International Monetary Fund, 8 Dec. 2016.

Gneezy, Uri, and Aldo Rustichini. 'A Fine Is a Price.' *The Journal of Legal Studies* 29.1 (2000): 1-17.

Keynes, John Maynard. *The General Theory of Employment, Interest and Money*. Basingstoke: Palgrave Macmillan, 2007.

Wetenschappelijke Raad voor het Regeringsbeleid. 'Samenleving en Financiële Sector in Evenwicht.' *WRR Rapporten* 96 (2016): 1-262.

Why an Open Dialogue is Needed

By Eelke de Jong

Introduction

T HE FINANCIAL SECTOR plays a key role in modern societies. It transfers money from savers to investors and thus enables the latter to realise profitable projects. This growth and development-enhancing role increases even further if the pool of resources is not restricted to a particular group; when an investor can borrow money from somebody he or she does not know. Consequently, a shift from a network-based financial system towards an at-arm's-length financial system is often observed in countries that show progress in terms of economic development. Banks play an important role in network-based systems, whereas financial markets dominate many at-arm's-length systems. An important difference between the two is that bilateral relations between a bank and its costumer are replaced by an anonymous transaction on the market. The most straightforward example is that of the bilateral agreement between bank and firm being replaced by a bond issued by the firm (with the help of the bank as advisor and trader) and subsequently traded on financial markets. The firm does not know the holders of the bond and has no direct relationship with them. This process of financialisation enables firms to attract more money than would have been possible otherwise. It increases the possibilities for both banks and firms of managing their financial risks. These positive effects of financial markets inspired William N. Goetzmann to entitle his history of finance 'Money changes everything: How finance made civilisation possible' (2016).

But the process of financialisation comes with significant downsides. First of all, replacing bilateral relations with anonymous ones requires new and more formal ways of acquiring information about a debtor's financial position. In a network-based system, trust in the debtor's willingness to repay and private judgement of the profitability of his business could act, at least in part, as a way to judge his creditworthiness. In at-arm's-length-based systems, such direct judgements are no longer possible or too expensive. Consequently, new ways of investigating a borrower's creditworthiness have to be found. Publicly available information and clear rules of (mis)conduct are often suggested as a solution. These rules have to be developed, implemented and upheld, which requires supervision bodies. Second, a financial market-based system assumes well-functioning financial markets, which implies a set of rules that prescribe who is allowed to act as a trader, and can therefore issue a bond or equity; as well as how to conduct transactions in a proper way. All these rules require institutions that supervise the activities and penalise misconduct. This means that operating a market-based system is quite costly, which explains why such systems are often found in developed economies. Finally, the fact that an at-arm's-length-based system facilitates agents to acquire funds implies that it has an internal tendency to stimulate overfunding. That is to say, investors obtain more money than they actually need, which means that their financial assets are not directly related to real economic activities. Periodic cycles of over-optimism and over-pessimism can easily occur and lead to financial crises. Serious financial crises can lead to an increase in unemployment and a downfall of trade and economic activity. The subprime credit crisis and the European debt crisis are recent examples of financial crises with large and long lasting negative consequences for real economic activity.

These very negative consequences of financial crises lead to the question of whether it is possible to mitigate the negative consequences of financial crises and of financialisation in particular. The aim of the current chapter is to deal with this question. It does not provide a framework for an ideal financial system, which can weather any and all storms. It is my conviction that such a system does not exist and therefore will never become reality. What I will do, however, is illustrate the following: in the past, experts have warned for certain economic developments that they perceived could easily lead to a financial crisis. This chapter will particularly address the reasons why these warnings were not taken seriously. Two major reasons are distinguished, namely political (un)willingness and cognitive bias. The run up to the subprime credit crisis is used as an example.

The setup of this chapter is as follows. The next section describes the two causes of the credit crisis. The third section assesses the reactions of politicians and experts on policy advice, and illustrates how political unwillingness and cognitive bias have played a role in the development, occurrence and aftermath of the subprime credit crisis. The fourth section presents some explanations for this political unwillingness and cognitive bias. The concluding section offers arguments in favour of an open debate, in order to mitigate the negative consequences of political unwillingness and cognitive bias.

Two main causes of the subprime credit crisis

A commonly held view is that the subprime credit crisis had two main causes. The first cause was the considerable number of disequilibria found worldwide on countries' balance of payments. The second cause concerns the high level of risk-taking by many participants in the Western financial system.

The disequilibria on the balance of payments were mainly found in the deficit on the current account of the United States and the surplus on this account of Asian countries and in particular China. These disequilibria reflected the fact that the United States (both government and private sector) spent far more money than they had earned. The reverse held for China. Since the Reagan administration, the United States (US) held a deficit on its current account. The Asian (Chinese) surpluses were inspired by the Asian crisis of 1997/1998 and started to increase from that period onwards. The way the International Monetary Fund had treated some Asian countries taught these countries that it would be wise to accumulate monetary reserves, which mainly consist of foreign assets. This would allow them to withstand future outflows of money. The accumulation of foreign assets can be accomplished by achieving surpluses on the current account over a long period of time. Chinese firms accumulated foreign money, in particular US dollars. They were unable (because of capital controls) or unwilling to invest these revenues in the United States, and for that reason they exchanged them for Chinese currency. The Chinese central bank was the counterparty to these Chinese firms and as such it acquired a huge sum of US dollars. Like almost all central banks, the Central Bank of China invested these funds in treasury bonds. Consequently, the price of US treasury bonds increased and their yields declined. At that time (which was the beginning of this century) the Bush administration welcomed this influx of dollars. The resulting low interest rate reduced the financial burden of the Iraq war.

The protracted low interest rate, however, generated the second main cause of the subprime credit crisis, namely excessive risk-taking. A low interest rate, lasting for a long period, usually means that those clients who need credit under normal conditions can easily obtain it. Their demand has been met, and banks are on the lookout for new customers to whom they can sell their products. These new customers are attracted by the low interest rate and the assumption that the interest rate will remain low for the foreseeable future. The creditworthiness of these new clients is low, so the banks' overall credit risk increases. Banks wish to mitigate this extra risk and invent ways to share it with other parties. This process of risk sharing introduces incentives to underestimate the risk. Since many parties share the risk, no single party has an incentive to investigate the 'lump sum' of risk for the entire group. Consequently, more risk is accepted than would be the case if any individual party had taken on the lump sum. This process continues until the assumption of everlasting low interest rates turns out to be false. The risks built up during the preceding period are revealed and a financial crisis ensues. This mechanism was in place in the period from the oil crisis (1973-1974) to the debt crisis of the 1980s. It also describes the events following the low interest rates of the first years of the current century.

In the period leading up to the subprime credit crisis, banks' new customers mainly consisted of American consumers without a permanent income and without any assets: No Income, No Job, No Assets (NINJAs). The loans they obtained were used to finance residential housing. This development was applauded by American politicians and stimulated by new regulations (cf. Schwartz 2009). The mortgage-backed securities functioned as the vehicle through which the resulting credit risk was shared among many partners.

Policy advice and reactions by politicians and experts

The previous section described the two main causes of the subprime credit crisis. Was there any policy advice in the period before the crisis that already mentioned these causes and urged policy makers to change their course? The short answer is: yes, there was.

Warnings for the potential detrimental effects of disequilibria on the balance of payments were already voiced in the mid-1990s. At the time, international economists were concerned about the protracted deficit on the US's current account. These deficits meant that the US transformed from a creditor to a debtor. How long would foreigners be willing to finance these deficits? What would happen when they refused to do this any longer? The current account would have to improve tremendously within a short period of time. This would require a huge depreciation of the US dollar. Given the pivotal role of the US dollar in the international financial system, what would be the consequences of a large and possibly abrupt depreciation of the dollar for the world financial system? The increasing surpluses on the current account of China during the first decade of this century intensified the relevance of these concerns, which were held by academics and central bankers alike. For example, the opening lines of a 2005 article by Obstfeld and Rogoff read as follows: 'This is the third in a series of papers we have written over the past five years about the growing U.S. current account deficit and the potentially sharp exchange rate movements any future adjustment toward current account balance might imply' (67). Central bankers raised their concerns as well.[2]

The International Monetary Fund (IMF) is the international institution that will be called upon in case disequilibria on balance of payments lead to international financial problems. Studying these imbalances is therefore one of their core tasks. The IMF management also knew that rebalancing these deficits would be a politically highly sensitive issue. In 2006, the IMF management decided to send a mission to the entities most responsible for global imbalances (Rajan 2010: 208-209). The managing director of the IMF hoped that smaller meetings would spawn more fruitful results than large international gatherings. All countries involved agreed with the IMF that 'the trade imbalances were a potential source of instability, and economic reforms were needed to bring them down before markets took fright or politicians decided to enter the fray with protectionist measures. But each country was then quick to point out why it was not responsible for the imbalances and why it would be so much easier for some other country to push a magic button to make them disappear' (Rajan 2010: 209).

In sum, the detrimental effects of current account imbalances were properly signalled by both academics and policy experts – and they did so well on time. The IMF urged politicians to take measures that would reduce the imbalances. Political will, however, was lacking. Governments confirmed the possible detrimental effects of imbalances on the current account. However, they refused to take the necessary measures to combat these effects. Instead, they pointed at others and said it was their responsibility.

The mechanism through which a low interest rate leads to an increase in risk within the financial system was less well understood. Nevertheless, it was identified and clearly explained by a number of mainstream economists. Chief among these was Raghuram G. Rajan, the main economist of the IMF in 2005. In August of that year, central bankers held their traditional annual gathering at Jackson Hole, Wyoming. This meeting would also serve as the farewell meeting for Allen Greenspan as chair of the Federal Reserve System. Rajan was asked to deliver a speech, and he decided to focus on the legacy of Greenspan's chairmanship. Some IMF staff members collected data for Rajan about the American financial system, which pointed to a situation far worse than he had expected. The development of the financial markets had occurred in such a way that huge risk increases had taken place within the system. In his talk, Rajan explained how the financial system had changed over the last decade. The fact that managers were at the time rewarded based on their relative performance had led to herd behaviour and investments in high risk assets. These are assets which show high return but also run the risk of huge losses; the so called tail risk. Rajan stressed that the practice of Special Purpose Vehicles (SPV) to finance mortgage-backed securities with short term loans could lead to large problems. An increase in the interest rate or a change in sentiment against property would decrease the value of mortgages and therefore the value of mortgage-backed securities. As a result, the SPV might be unable to refinance its assets. 'If banks also face credit losses and there is uncertainty about where those losses are located, only the very unimpeachable banks will receive the supply of liquidity fleeing other markets. If these banks also lose confidence in their liquidity-short brethren, the inter-bank market could freeze up, and one could well have a full blown financial crisis' (Rajan 2005: 26). Rajan's conclusion in August 2005 was this: 'We should prepare for the low probability but highly costly downturn' (Rajan 2005: 37). The costs of this crisis could be so extreme that they might appear to be unbearable for the present generation. Two years later, the subprime credit crisis developed exactly in the way Rajan had suggested.

How did the public of central bankers and financial experts react to these prophetical words? The usual questions were raised. Some were outright critical. Larry Summers, for example, was of the opinion that 'the basic slightly Luddite premise of the paper' was 'largely misguided'.[3] In 2010, Rajan wrote about this experience as follows: 'I did not, however, foresee the reaction from the normally polite conference audience. I exaggerate only a bit when I say I felt like an early Christian who had wandered into a convention of half-starved lions. As I walked away from the podium (…), I felt some unease. (…) it was because the critics seemed to be ignoring what was going on before their eyes' (Rajan 2010: 3). This is exactly what I mean by cognitive bias. The audience attending Rajan's speech was caught up in the idea that the American financial system was the best the world had ever had – and that it was also the best the world could ever have. They could not change their mind set to incorporate critique on this system. This appeared to be a generally held view: as far as I know, international newspapers did not report on Rajan's prophetic speech.

Political unwillingness and cognitive bias

The previous section illustrated that both political unwillingness and cognitive bias have played a role in neglecting valuable advice that, if implemented, could have reduced or even prevented the disastrous subprime credit crisis.

What, then, explains the political neglect of valuable advice? An important explanatory factor is that often the costs of measures to be implemented are both upfront and, to a certain degree, known. Meanwhile, benefits of these measures are only revealed later in time and may be unknown or at least less precisely predictable. The mismatch in time of costs and benefits is particularly important for elected politicians. In many countries, politicians' mandate expires after four or five years. In effect, this period is even shorter if we take into account the time it takes to get new legislation through parliament and to have new measures implemented. Consequently, chances are high that the costs have to be incurred during the period the government is in office, while the benefits are received during the reign of the next government. As a result, a politician who is implementing necessary but costly (that is, unpopular) measures risks being outvoted during the next elections. The German Bundeskanzler Schröder is a good example in this regard. His government implemented necessary labour market reforms (Harz I – IV). During the next election, Schröder's party (the Social Democrats) was outvoted and his successor, Bundeskanzlerin Merkel, reaped the benefits of Schröder's measures for three elections in a row.

Another reason for political reluctance to implement necessary policies can be found in the so-called negativity bias. The negativity bias is the psychological phenomenon where people attach much more significance to negative events than to positive ones. The negativity bias explains, for example, practices of blaming and loss aversion. For politicians, it implies that a wait-and-see strategy is preferred to an active approach of solving potential problems before they occur. The latter strategy could result in costs that will without doubt be blamed on the politicians' course of action.

Until now I have assumed that the costs and benefits of policy imple-mentation are known. In reality, this tends not to be the case. Suppose that in the period 2005 – 2006 the governments of major countries would have taken the IMF's advice to heart and implemented measures to reduce the current account imbalances. This would have meant that the

US government would have reduced expenditures in the US (both official and private), and that China would have relied on its own currency rather than investing in the foreign dollar. Let us assume that these measures had resulted in a much milder crisis than the subprime credit crisis that actually took place. Who would ever have known? The counterfactual event, in that case, would have been the subprime credit crisis. That crisis would not have happened and would have remained unimaginable, as it was before the year 2007. Politicians could then never have pointed out the great services they carried out for the world and their voter base, because nobody would have been aware of this counterfactual event.

Cognitive bias has been put forward as another explanation for neglecting policy advice. This bias results from the fact that human beings use their current cognitive frame for interpreting new information. The reason for this is that the world is too complex for a human being: we rely on a framework of familiarity to explain new events. This cognitive frame is developed over the years through education and experience. The adolescent years are often regarded as crucial in this respect. A systematic and enduring way of training can result in human beings who 'will accept their deformation as the natural state of affairs and even take pride in it, as Chinese women once did in their crippled feet' according to psychologist Milton R. Sapirstein (cited in Sommer, 2013, p. 185). Group thinking seems to have been an important factor in explaining the neglect of Rajan's policy advice (cf. Wagner and Lamdany 2011).

Concluding remarks

The previous sections have emphasised the role of political unwillingness and cognitive bias in refusing to act on valuable policy advice. The relevance of these factors for neglecting policy advice that, if implemented, could have prevented the subprime credit crisis or softened its consequences raises the following question: how can one reduce the influence of political unwillingness and cognitive bias? My suggestion is that an open mind is key in this respect. No one knows exactly how the economy works or what the future will look like. However, we can learn from one another. This requires a willingness to listen to others, even if the other has different (political) interests or represents a minority view. We must try to understand what the world looks like from the perspective of someone else. We must check the logical arguments offered by the other, and engage with the empirical relevance of the minority's view. In sum, we must arrive at an open-minded debate on the causes and consequences of recent developments and on possible policy measures. I would recommend an open discussion between representatives from academics, the financial industry and the government. This is precisely the aim of the Socires series of conferences and dialogues that were organised under the header 'Ethics and Finance; The Finance – State – Society Triangle in Europe'. Participants in these events came from sectors relevant to the debate: they were bankers, (institutional) investors, companies, politicians, public officers and policy advisors from selected European countries. I hope that these events have broadened the participants' views, have helped them understand other positions, and have opened their eyes to neglected aspects of the wider debate.

1. Many of the ideas described in this chapter have been presented before (see De Jong 2017). Additionally, this publication was made possible through the support of a grant from Templeton World Charity Foundation, Inc. The opinions expressed in this publication are those of the author and do not necessarily reflect the views of Templeton World Charity Foundation, Inc.

2. See for example the Dutch Central Bank's annual report for 2003: '[d]e belangrijkste risico's voor de wereldeconomie, en niet het minst voor Europa, liggen bij de betalingsbalansonevenwichtigheden' (De Nederlandsche Bank 2004).

3. This remark was made during the general discussion at the Jackson Hole conference.

Bibliography

De Jong, Eelke. *Laat een Crisis Niet Nodig Zijn. Pleidooi voor een Open Debat.* Nijmegen: Valkhof Pers, 2017.

De Nederlandsche Bank. *Jaarverslag over 2003.* Amsterdam: DNB, 2004.

Goetzmann, William N. *Money Changes Everything. How Finance Made Civilization Possible.* Princeton, NJ: University Press, 2016.

Obstfeld, Maurice, and Kenneth S. Rogoff. 'Global Current Account Imbalances and Exchange Rate Adjustments.' *Brookings Papers on Economic Activity* 1 (2005): 67-123.

Rajan, Raghuram G. 'Has Financial Development Made the World Riskier?' *National Bureau of Economic Research Working Papers* 11728 (2005): 1-42.

Rajan, Raghuram G. *Fault Lines. How Hidden Fractures Still Threaten the World Economy.* Princeton, NJ: University Press, 2010.

Schwartz, H. W. *Subprime Nation, American Power, Global Capital, and the Housing Bubble.* Ithaca, NY, and London: Cornell University Press, 2009.

Sommer, Elyse. *Smiles Dictionary.* Canton, MI: Visible Ink Press, second edition, 2013.

Wagner, Nancy Louise, and Ruben Lamdany. *IMF Performance in the Run-Up to the Financial and Economic Crisis. IMF Surveillance in 2004-07.* Washington, DC: IMF, 2011.

Complexity, Culture, and Bank Privatisations

By Roland Kupers

THE CASUAL JUSTIFICATION for the privatisation of banks nationalised during the 2008 financial crisis – among which ABN AMRO – is often simply that 'they belong in the market'. Through this somewhat circular argument, we may be missing an opportunity to change, and indeed even improve, the system of finance. When one applies a complex-systems lens to finance, other options come into view that might be considered. However, those options cannot become part of the policy debate, if this debate is not preceded by a conversation on the nature of the system, and on its uncertainties.

A brief recap of the events surrounding ABN AMRO. In 2007, the Royal Bank of Scotland, Fortis and Banco Santander pooled their resources and together bought Dutch bank ABN AMRO for the sum of €72 billion. They then proceeded to divide the bank into segments. During the financial crisis, in October 2008, the Dutch government nationalised the various Dutch assets belonging to the bank. Along with further funding provided to the ailing bank, the total cost of this manoeuvre would raise the national debt burden of the Netherlands by some €30 billion (Centraal Bureau voor de Statistiek 2015). In addition, the British and Spanish governments would need to spend billions to reinforce banks of their own – those that had absorbed pieces of the former ABN AMRO. Understandably, this created strong pressure on subsequent Dutch governments to recoup some of these costs through an early privatisation. While the pressure was essentially political in nature, the argument presented was a simple one: the bank belongs back in the market.

This argument sidesteps an essential debate on the systemic aspects of finance. It also misses a potential opportunity to improve it. Unpacking these arguments allows us to explore our assumptions about the financial system, and to see what other options may exist.

Markets are social constructs

Free market advocates often present markets as something of a natural phenomenon, where an invisible hand organises things. The fewer rules and regulations, the better it will function, so the argument goes. But markets are not natural systems. They are a human creation, within which self-organisation occurs. The market is designed through rules - and we can reflect on its design, its path dependencies and its history. It is this design and history that largely determines the type of self-organisation that occurs within the complex system of the market, including the occurrence of repeated financial crises. This is not to express any political position on privatisation; it is simply an encouragement for precision.

It is not just that the financial system is prone to crises; those crises have also had a deep influence. The Economist published an extensive report a few years ago, entitled 'The Slumps That Shaped Modern Finance'. The report lays out how finance is not merely prone to crises, but is in fact shaped by them (The Economist 2014). It describes how five previous, devastating financial slumps - starting with America's first crash in 1792 and ending with the world's biggest in 1929 - highlight two big trends in financial evolution. The first is that the institutions that provide the scaffolding for the system, such as central banks, deposit insurance companies and stock exchanges, are not the products of careful design in calm times, but have often been cobbled together at the bottom of financial cliffs. The second is more troubling: each and every crisis ends by entrenching public backing for private markets, and those parts of finance that are deemed essential are given more state support. It is an approach that may appear sensible and even reassuring at a time of crisis, but every single time more risk is transferred to the state, and less risk remains with private capital. Post-crisis, some of this transfer may be reversed, but never all of it. The consequence of this ratcheting mechanism is that investors are increasingly insulated from risk.

It all starts with the crisis of 1792, when a young Etonian called William Duer essentially blew up the financial market and ended up in prison. He had in fact conned so many people that he described prison as the safest place for him to be. The first secretary of the treasury of the US,

Alexander Hamilton, then bailed out the financial system and followed up on this by carrying out a number of operations similar to the ones we witnessed in 2008. The basis of his operations was to gradually socialise more risk while continuing to fully privatise returns.

This analysis is simply the description of the outcome of a series of decisions taken over the course of more than two centuries, each of them with its own internal logic. Cumulatively, however, those decisions have shaped the financial industry as we know it today. As a result, it is simply not accurate to refer to a free market in finance the way it is commonly done in policy debates. Meanwhile, the 'existence' of a free market remains the essential justification today for the privatisation of banks.

Complexity

In a 2014 book (*Complexity and the Art of Public Policy*), David Colander and I discussed the origin of this constrained view of markets that underpins many policy narratives. We met at a climate policy conference in Berlin, and shared a plane ride home. We were both uncomfortable with the way solutions were being framed for climate issues. Some people argued for lots of state regulation in order to mitigate excessive warming, while others argued that market forces would deliver more efficient solutions, as long as they were given the right incentives. As with the privatisation of ABN AMRO, there seemed to be only two possible solutions: state or market, with the latter option being the default one.

The reason David and I were uncomfortable with the market/state dichotomy is that we both have a deep interest in the science of complex systems. Complexity has developed over the past several decades, to the point where most university faculties now offer complexity programmes. Complexity is one of the core themes of Dutch research funding (Vermeer 2014).

Unfortunately, the discipline was given an awkward name. To many people, complexity is a negative thing. There are consultants who dedicate themselves to the elimination of complexity. Let me therefore first elaborate on the term itself. In Latin, 'plexus' means 'to braid'. One could associate the discipline of complexity with the image of a fair maiden with meticulously braided hair or, say, Julia Timoshenko with her signature braids. Complexity is the science of braided or interconnected systems. They are spaghetti-like structures such as your immune system, a city, or a financial system.

We can contrast the idea of 'complex' with that of 'complicated': a garden is complicated, while a tropical forest is complex. If you remove a flowerbed from your garden, it performs just fine. The garden is really just a collection of plants with no essential interconnections between them. The whole is exactly the sum of its parts. Or as Blaise Pascal famously said: 'Je tiens impossible de connaître les parties sans connaître le tout, non plus que de connaître le tout sans connaître particulièrement les parties'[1] (2015: 165). In a tropical forest, on the other hand, plants and animals depend on each other for survival. Remove a few species, and the whole system could collapse. The system's properties are defined both by its parts and by interconnections between those parts. The whole is more than the sum of its parts, when considered in a scientifically precise sense.

The story of the discipline of complex systems started in 1986 when Citibank sponsored a conference to come up with a better theory of finance and economics. Ken Arrow and Murray Gell-Mann, Nobel Laureates in Economics and Physics, each picked a team of leading thinkers. They assembled in Santa Fe, New Mexico, to explain their theories to one another. The conclusion was properly formulated by one of the physicists present, who described economics as a 'Cuban car, lovingly maintained, but with hopelessly outdated technology' (Beinhocker 2006). This was in 1986. Since then, considerable progress has been made in analysing the economy as a complex system. Very little of that, however, has thus far had an impact on policy considerations (Arthur 2014). We are still all too often in the 'Cuban car' era.

Let us consider a number of examples that demonstrate how taking a complex systems lens changes policy choices. Imagine that the network of banks is like the garden from our earlier example. If all the individual flowers are healthy, the garden is healthy as well. This means that the central gardener, or in this case the central banker, must watch over the health of all individual banks to ensure the health of the overall system.

However, if the banking system is more like a tropical forest, we are dealing with a different matter entirely. The central bank must then be accountable for the stability of the system as a whole, with less concern for the individual banks (May, Levin, and Sugihara 2008).

Of course, the network aspects of the financial system were both knowable and known before 2008 (cf. Pröpper, Van Lelyveld, and Heijmans 2008). However, it was not until after the crisis that the full deficiency of financial modelling was articulated. In 2010, Jean-Claude Trichet stated that 'scientists have developed sophisticated tools for analysing complex dynamic systems in a rigorous way. These models have proved helpful in understanding many important but complex phenomena. [...] I am hopeful that central banks can also benefit from these insights in developing tools to analyse financial markets and monetary policy transmission' (Trichet 2010).

European banks are subject to stress tests, but these tests treat interconnections only as an additional factor to the health of individual banks. This disregards an essential element, namely that the network structure creates complex feedback loops between banks. Equally, the ongoing debate on the right level of leverage presumes that our understanding of the system is such, that *it is actually possible* to decide whether 13% of leverage is better than 4%, or even than 40%. However, while the increase of leverage requirements is a pragmatically motivated improvement, we do not actually know whether it is adequate. Our models are out of date. No one is to blame for this: it is just the current state of the art. Acknowledging this uncertainty is essential to progress.

Complexity science has made some headway, but not nearly enough. Famous physicist Stephen Hawking opined that complexity will be the main science of the 21st century. As such, there is still time. At the very least, however, we should stop justifying policy decisions that are based on models we know to be inadequate.

Developing a better understanding of the way the financial system works requires us to ask new questions. For instance, triggered by the steady flow of large fines and criminal convictions, Ernst Fehr and colleagues at the University of Zurich set out to explore whether bankers are more dishonest than average citizens. What they found is both surprising and interesting: 'Employees of a large international bank behaved by-and-large as honestly as the rest of us. But in tests designed to mimic the competitive nature of their profession, many of the bankers began to act dishonestly' (Cohn, Fehr, and Maréchal 2014). In other words, you can trust a banker during a private dinner in the evening, but certainly not at the bank during the day. People's social norms are not fixed, but are largely formed based on the individual's context. What Fehr and his colleagues found indicated that banks foster and spread perverse social norms. Meanwhile, traditional economic models assume that social norms and the preferences of individuals are fixed. While it is no secret that this is a crude approximation at best, this assumption is grounded in the fact that it makes models mathematically more tractable. It will require innovative complex systems models to start to contend with context-dependent preferences.

Another complexity insight is that diverse systems are more resilient under uncertain circumstances (De Nederlandsche Bank 2015). Diversity applies at multiple scales, ranging from individuals to companies. The Dutch financial system has one of the highest concentrations and lowest diversity rates of banks in the European Union. Its financial sector is also relatively large (European Central Bank 2017). These are not the characteristics of a stable and resilient system.

Of course, banks do not exist in isolation. They have also initiated substantial change programmes of their own accord since the 2008 crisis. This applies both to central banks and private banks, such as ABN AMRO. The latter is today also a very different company from when it was sold in 2007: it is smaller, more local, and has an evolving internal culture.

The crises of 1720, 1792, 1825, 1837, 1929, and 2008 show how financial markets are all too often the result of design through panic. There are scant grounds for describing them as truly free markets that are best left to flourish on their own. Our fundamental understanding of the financial system is rapidly evolving, but between cultural issues, diversity, and size, the Dutch financial sector cannot reasonably be described as having achieved a desirable and stable end state. One of the roles of the government is to ensure a healthy financial system. The privatisation of a formerly nationalised bank – for example, ABN AMRO – would require far more rigorous argumentation as to how this would contribute to a less risky financial system. The public is not well served with a limited justification for a return to 'business as usual'.

Privatisation has clear benefits for the finances of the state – however, the price of the potential loss of a powerful instrument of reform has not been quantified.

What are the alternatives?

Central banks could be more explicitly tasked with managing the health of the network of banks, rather than only looking after individual banks. Fortunately, more progressive central banks such as DNB, EUR and UK all have complexity programmes up and running, and are actively exploring these now models of governance. Policy makes will also have to adjust their perspectives.

The fact that so much risk has been effectively removed from the financial system – by shifting much of the entrepreneurial risk to the state – raises the question of how 'private' the banking industry really is. The simple statement that the state is not a banker may well be an oxymoron.

Consider a norms policy for banks. We met William Duer, the culprit of the 1792 crisis, and may assume that he acquired even worse personal norms during his time in prison. Similarly, banks as institutions seem to stimulate wrong behaviour. If the state controlled and owned an important player in the financial system, this could be an excellent tool to address this problem across the sector; owning a bank (as state) would be a tool to evolve norms. This is by no means a simple task, but it is an essential one.

A complex system requires diversity in order to remain healthy. A system like the Dutch, with a small number of large private banks, makes for a poor structure. How can we increase diversity? We must vary both size and ownership structure. Again, owning a bank is helpful to the state, especially if new insights lead to the desire to create smaller banks with differing business models.

From a complex systems perspective, it is clear that privatisation should be preceded by a far richer debate on the nature and dynamics of the financial system. Furthermore, an explanation must be given on how privatisation would contribute to the construction of a more resilient banking system.

What we currently know about the nature of systems indicates that adding yet another big private player to the Dutch banking system most likely will not increase its resilience. It also means a missed opportunity to actually re-engineer the system from within. The consequences for the future are likely to be either more heavy-handed regulation, or waiting for the next bail-out.

1. Trans: 'I hold it equally impossible to know the parts without knowing the whole, as it is to know the whole without knowing all the parts'.

Bibliography

Arthur, W. B. *Complexity and the Economy.* Oxford: University Press, 2014.

Beinhocker, Eric D. *The Origin of Wealth: Evolution, Complexity, and the Radical Remaking of Economics.* Boston: Harvard Business School Press, 2006.

Centraal Bureau voor de Statistiek. 'Staatsschuld door Overname Fortis / ABN AMRO 30 Miljard Hoger.' *CBS.* CBS, 20 Nov. 2015.

Cohn, A., Fehr, E., and M.A. Maréchal. 'Business culture and dishonesty in the banking industry.' *Nature* 516.7529 (2014): 86–89.

Colander, David, and Roland Kupers. *Complexity and the Art of Public Policy – Changing Society from the Bottom-Up.* Princeton: University Press, 2014.

De Nederlandsche Bank. 'Perspective on the Structure of the Dutch Banking Sector. Efficiency and Stability through Competition and Diversity.' *DNB Study* (2015): 1-64.

European Central Bank. *Report on Financial Structures.* Frankfurt am Main: ECB, 2017.

May, R. M, Levin, S. A., and G. Sugihara. 'Complex Systems: Ecology for Bankers.' *Nature* 451.7181 (2008): 893-895.

Pascal, Blaise. *Pensées.* CreateSpace Independent Publishing Platform, 2015.

Pröpper, M., van Lelyveld, I., and R. Heijmans. 'Toward a Network Description of Interbank Payment Flows.' *DNB Working Papers* 177 (2008): 1-27.

The Economist. 'The Slumps that Shaped Modern Finance.' *The Economist.* The Economist, April 2014.

Trichet, J.C. 'Reflections on the Nature of Monetary Policy Non-Standard Measures and Finance Theory.' Central Banking Conference, European Central Bank, 18 Nov. 2010, Frankfurt.

Vermeer, Bram, ed. *Grip on Complexity. Directions for Future Complexity Research.* The Hague: Netherlands Organisation for Scientific Research, 2014.

On the Economic Trinity[1]

By Govert Buijs

Introduction

IN THIS CONTRIBUTION I will elaborate on the doctrine of the trinity. You may have heard of this doctrine as a kind of theological delicacy in Christianity. Do not worry – that is not my brief here. What I wish to address is the *economic trinity*, that is to say: the trinity of the contract – or for that matter any transaction that takes place on the market.

My thesis is that in mainstream economic thinking, as well as in general practice, we have come to misunderstand transactions as simple, one-dimensional operations. In this way we have forgotten what it takes for a market to work well. In fact, we may undermine the very preconditions for the market. In that sense, we have started to act as parasites – which generally do not end very well, as the parasite has a tendency to consume his host. If we lack a proper understanding of market transactions and act on that understanding, we may start to thwart the proper functioning of the market. It is exactly this, which may give, and likely has already given, rise to feelings of alienation among the wider public. It has even led to public outrage, the effects of which are now permeating our political system.

It will be my claim that reflection on the mentioned economic trinity shows a path to an agenda of renewal for (financial) organisations and their employees. Towards the end of this contribution, I will elaborate on six key elements of this agenda.

Three kinds of contracts in each transaction

Every market transaction involves three contracts that are concluded simultaneously. The first contract is the most visible one and is almost always committed to paper. This could be as simple as a receipt received in the supermarket. The contract describes the concrete 'tit-for-tat': a jar of peanut butter for €1.50. However, this first contract is always accompanied by a second one, which is not written down; it is an implicit

69

contract, contract II, which actually makes possible contract I.

This second contract states that both contractors in contract I make a promise not to cheat on each other. The existence of contract II can easily be understood, namely *ex negativo*: if I would know at the point of conclusion of contract I that the other partner is cheating on me, the transaction will not proceed, but will be cancelled. As such, contract II is tacitly presupposed in contract I. The first we can call the 'formal-legal contract', the second is the 'trust contract'.

And then there is a third contract. The very second the two contractors conclude their transaction they also enter into a contract with the society they are in. They assume that society will respect their mutual agreement. Above all, however, they also assume that society will ensure that effective redress is possible if one of the partners fails to live up to the terms of the contract. As such, any agreement, be it written or verbal, implicitly refers to a society in which there is a rule of law: one that serves as the background and the foundation, enabling people to produce and consume, to wheel and to deal. This also means that both parties implicitly situate themselves in the community and are therefore committed to the wellbeing of society. This third contract is the 'social contract' or 'civil contract'. It implies the promise to at the very least refrain from harming the legal and social order; and positively formulated it implies that one actually acknowledges the duty to sustain and promote this order.[2]

These are three different contracts, yet at the same time they are one – hence I call them a trinity. If one of the three is denied or obscured, no transaction can take place, at least not on a sustained basis.

Of course, it is possible to shift the relative weight between the three contracts. If contract II is downplayed, it can be compensated by high transaction costs. The first contract becomes a mountain of paper and a matter to be dealt with by lawyers and solicitors. If one minimises the social contract, society can only respond with ever increasing regulations that eventually may undermine the creative freedom that the market requires from an economic perspective. Yet even then, the trinity can never be ignored completely. After all, if ever it turns out that the parties involved in a contract have violated one of its three 'sub'-contracts, anger and frustration will follow and further transactions become very difficult.

The parties will be in big trouble and may even risk liquidation – clear examples of this are Arthur Andersen and Enron. And we have seen such anger in the last decade: there has been great public outrage at the role of the banks in the financial crisis.

From Occupy to populism and beyond…

On a socio-psychological and political level, our society is experiencing hectic times. Many citizens feel insecure and unprotected. One of the most influential social science advisors of the Dutch government, Paul Schnabel, expressed this sentiment in his famous one-liner: '*I* am fine, but *we* are not' (cf. 2018). Individual wellbeing is at odds with the way people feel society is doing.

There is a widespread feeling of betrayal: the societal contract has been undermined by some of the parties involved. The Occupy movement was an expression of this sentiment. Feelings of distrust have acquired even more force by their adoption into the views of populist movements worldwide. The close relationship between the leftist Occupy movement and right-wing populism was underlined by a CNN commentator in early 2017, when he noted that Donald Trump's inauguration speech could almost have been written by Bernie Sanders. The latter might have mentioned 'Wall Street' a few times, while Trump considered 'Washington' the origin and epitome of all evil.

We do live in an age of deeply felt distrust in institutions, ranging from state to church, from housing corporations to health care institutions, and from banks to educational institutions. Why? 'Burgerschap', the Dutch word for 'citizenship', is derived from 'burcht', shelter or castle. Institutions give shelter to people. In this basic role, many institutions are failing today.

I believe this brief analysis makes visible the contours of an agenda of restoration and innovation that representatives of financial institutions and society must explore. Let me summarise current events as well as this agenda of renewal in six key points.

1. Acknowledge that the financial sector has played a key role in growing distrust

Research by Funke et al (2016) shows that in the period between 1870 and 2014, a political crisis almost always occurred within a few years of a financial crisis. These political crises were characterised by populist movements – or worse. The financial sector has created and/or stimulated the current post-crisis distrust in two ways. First, it has tarnished or even destroyed its own century-old reputation of reliability and trustworthiness. Second, in its gargantuan growth, the sector has become an entirely self-contained 'new economy'; one that is larger than the 'first economy', but with far less transparency. The financial sector is a globally operating, massive force of economic energy that nobody can curb or control.

Here we touch upon the issue of 'financialisation': the immensely increased role of the financial sector we experience every day in universities, health care institutions, and in politics. It seems that the only debates that matter today deal with money issues. In the background, debt and risk management issues are often involved.

The lesson is this: we must curb our dependence on finance and our addiction to debt.

2. Pay new attention to the forgotten second and third contracts

As explained above, every market transaction consists of three contracts: the manifest, or formal, contract, the trust contract and the social contract. It is essential that the second and third contract once again receive all the attention they deserve – in theory, but even more in practice. This implies, for example, that the reliability and trustworthiness of banks in the relationship with customers must again become indubitable. Banks should also be aware of their societal role and significance; that is to say: they should live up to the third contract.

3. Develop new ethics ...

Much attention has been given in recent years to the personal ethics of employees of (financial) institutions. Employees must develop virtues, identify moral dilemmas, and know how to deal with these dilemmas. In itself, this is a positive development. Yet we should not fool ourselves with fancy language, or have wrong expectations of employees in the financial sector – that they are to become ethical virtuosi that always stand on a moral high ground. They are only weak, vulnerable, and impressionable human beings – like everyone else. The new ethics we require should not only give attention to the moral demands that people must meet in order to be 'virtuous', but also (and perhaps more importantly) to phenomena such as moral weakness, transgression, and forgiveness.

4. ... and new systems

It is rather a risk to expect too much from employees' personal ethics. We are all weak: sometimes inadvertently, sometimes because we are inclined to do evil. It is therefore equally important to pay attention to the moral design of systems and organisational cultures. How do our incentive systems work? What type of behaviour is rewarded (financially, but also in terms of career opportunities), and what behaviour is punished? What is the organisational culture?

At the end of the day, what is true leadership? Does it focus on financial profit, quality of services, customer satisfaction, or societal responsibility? How does the organisation as a whole deal with its duty to protect customers?

5. Find a new definition of relevant actors: true stakeholders

Many problems today have their roots in an extremely limited definition of who the actual stakeholders of a (financial) company are. Many companies have given their shareholders an all-dominant position. This has come at the expense of, for example, customers. It is particularly regrettable that this has happened to banks, for they commonly originate from citizens' initiatives, such as cooperatives. They oftentimes were never private market organisations to begin with; rather, they were civil organisations that were explicitly designed to provide protection to people. Many banks have become parasitic outgrowths of their own origins. As such, a new identification of true stakeholders must take place.

6. Identify what we should consider the telos, or ultimate goal, of our economy

Why do we have an economy? This simple question is hardly discussed in contemporary economic science. If the question would receive a clear answer, it could be possible to give positive direction to economic behavior. If we identify what it is that we are doing and what we are doing it for, we can judge whether we are on track. Gradually, indeed, more substantive answers are started to being given, often relating to 'happiness' of 'human flourishing'. This implies that the key question that must be asked by financial institutions is as follows: do we – or does the process of financialisation, which we have promoted in the past – actually contribute to human happiness and/or human flourishing?

In conclusion

My contribution started by reflecting on the economic trinity of transaction, trust, and society. To restore this trinity is indeed almost a religious act, in the sense that it presupposes something like a 'conversion' or change of ways. If there is one truth found in almost all classical religious and in philosophical traditions, it is this: conversion, a change of heart, is not easy – but it is certainly feasible.

---

1. This publication was made possible through the support of a grant from Templeton World Charity Foundation, Inc. The opinions expressed in this publication are those of the author and do not necessarily reflect the views of Templeton World Charity Foundation, Inc.

2. The Value Added Tax in many countries can be seen as an explicit acknowledgement of the third contract, but the thrust of the contract goes further than that: it refers to a full acknowledgement of the legal and social order in the country.

Bibliography

Funke, M, et al. 'Going to Extremes. Politics after Financial Crises, 870-2014.' *European Economic Review* 88 (2016): 227-260.

Schnabel, Paul. *Met Mij Gaat het Goed, Met Ons Gaat het Slecht. Het Gevoel van Nederland.* Amsterdam: Prometheus, 2018.

PART 2

Finance and Relations

Finance: A Relational Perspective

By Lans Bovenberg

THIS PAPER DESCRIBES finance from a relational point of view. To do so, it employs elements from a new method to teach economics as the science of human cooperation. The goal of this education reform in secondary education is to do *more* with *less*. My first objective is to teach a *more* relational view of man than the rational, individualistic *homo economicus* (section 1). My second objective is to make economics *less* complex and *less* fragmented by relating various economic concepts to each other. In particular, young people will learn that economics is a discipline of human cooperation and hope. To that end, I introduce economics in three steps: 'in balance', 'out of balance' and 'more balance' (section 2). I illustrate the method by applying it to finance in sections 3, 4 and 5 (with, respectively, in/out of/more balance). Section 6 argues in favour of more emphasis on relational rather than transactional modes of governance in finance. A shift away from liquidity and debt finance to more equity finance is called for. Section 7 provides my conclusion.

1. A relational view of humans

Model of homo economicus

Economics education is still to a large extent based on a belief in the model of the autonomous *homo economicus*. By relying mainly on this model of rational, a-moral man, economics education biases the perception of students. The assumption that people are motivated only by selfishness results in fear of greed. It makes people afraid to commit, and as a result it leads people to look only after their own interests (Grant 2013). This model also biases governance towards extrinsic motivation. In particular, in order to stimulate cooperation, institutions rely on top-down control and extrinsic, financial incentives rather than on intrinsic motivations (Bowles, 2016).

More diversity in models and the art of model selection
To be clear, I am not arguing to eliminate the model of the rational, self-interested man from the high school curriculum. What I argue for is teaching a richer diversity of models and, most importantly, the art of model selection: which model is most appropriate in which circumstance? The model of the *homo economicus* can be a good approximation for behaviour in competitive markets with many potential traders, in which people rely on short-term, anonymous transactions rather than durable, face-to-face relationships. At the same time, people spend most of their time in small associations and partnerships. In these contexts, a relational view of man is more realistic than the view of the *homo economicus*.

Bounded rationality
Recent academic developments in the discipline of economics support more relational models of human behaviour. Taking the scarcity of cognitive abilities seriously, behavioural economics shows that people make systematic mistakes – especially when dealing with intertemporal choices and decisions under uncertainty. Indeed, in order to make sensible decisions in these contexts, people rely not only on their intellect but also on intuition and emotions. They also rely on trust in others (Kahneman, 2011).

Social preferences: people value fairness
Recent developments in economics demonstrate that individual preferences are to be understood socially, in two respects. First, people derive respect, identity and purpose from contributing to a larger whole that transcends their own life (Akerlof and Kranton 2010). They intrinsically value fairness, justice, and the quality of relationships, including mutual trust and reciprocity (Ariely, 2012).

Preferences are affected by others
A second way in which individual preferences are socially bound is that personal values can be affected, stimulated and activated by others, and the social context in which people live. More virtues can gradually be

acquired, resulting in a richer and more fulfilling life. People tend to underestimate the possibilities of themselves and others to change and evolve their behaviour (Wilkinson and Klaes, 2012).

Social preferences create opportunities...
Social preferences imply that people interact not only through markets and prices; they also affect each other's preferences and beliefs (Van Winden, 2016). In the presence of externalities and other market failures, social preferences can help internalise externalities, ensuring that people do not take advantage of the opportunity to reap personal benefit at the expense of others.

...and threats
However, a more relational view of human beings does not imply that people are saints: jealousy, conformism, social pressure, and vengefulness also originate in the relational character of humans. Moreover, the desire to belong to one group can block empathy for those outside that group.

Endogenous preferences create opportunities and threats
Shaping values yields both opportunities and dangers. With regards to opportunities, both parents and schools are able to not only teach kids cognitive skills but also to build their character and virtues (Sachs, 2015). As regards the dangers, people may try to affect the values and beliefs of others in order to benefit themselves at the expense of others. 'Phishing for phools' is therefore an important governance challenge (Akerlof and Shiller, 2015).

2. Economics in three steps

The English word 'economics' originates in the Greek word *oikonomíā*, which means rules (*nómos*) of the household (*oîkos*). Indeed, the discipline of economics involves governing (i.e. ruling) households. 'Household' should be understood in the broad sense of the word, in that it refers to cooperative arrangements (i.e. economies) such as a family, corporation, a country, or the world as a whole. Economics thus studies the rules ('laws') of fruitful human cooperation. It is about governing cooperation.

One narrative provides coherence

A narrative of hope provides more coherence to economics education, thereby preparing students to balance objectives and interests when governing their own household or other cooperative arrangements in which they participate. This story of hope consists of three steps: *in balance, out of balance* and *more balance*. In a medical metaphor, these three steps correspond to (1) the ideal of health; (2) the diagnosis of illness; (3) the prescription of medicine. This single, unified analytical framework makes economics less complex.

Hope

Economics in three steps involves hope. Hope starts from the ideal of human dignity and human flourishing. As a second step, hope is realistic about the limitations of the rationality, consciousness and morality of human beings. It thus acknowledges that the current situation is far from ideal. Finally, hope engages in action to bring the actual situation closer to the ideal. At the same time, it recognises that human endeavours face serious obstacles and remain imperfect.

Hope versus naivety and cynicism

Hope is the third, narrow road between the broad roads of naivety and cynicism. The road of naïve optimism denies the darkness of the world; it maintains that all is well in the world. As such, it is false hope: opium for the people. The road of cynicism, in contrast, argues that the world is worthless and hopeless.

3. Finance in balance

The balance of win-win in justice and ethics

The main principle guiding human interaction is mutual benefit, or the balance of win-win. The balance of win-win is at the heart of justice: giving all people their rightful, fair share. The win-win principle – treating others the way you want to be treated yourself – is also the golden rule of ethics. Economics – on the one hand – and ethics and justice – on the other – are two sides of the same coin of the balance of win-win.

1+1=3 as the miracle of economics
Recognising this unity in diversity, this paper focuses on developing an economic perspective on the balance of win-win. The miracle of economics is that together we can achieve more than each of us individually. Cooperation yields more than the sum of the parts: 1+1=3. In the language of economics, life is not a zero-sum game. This main insight of economics conflicts with the intuition of many.

Difference and sharing create value
Two foundations undergird the miracle of 1+1=3. The first involves diversity. The more partners differ in talents and preferences, the greater becomes the potential value that is added through cooperation. Difference (-) creates value added (+): - = +. The second foundation involves sharing the fruits of cooperation. If all stakeholders gain, trust grows and all want to participate. Accordingly, division (:) of value multiplies (x) value so that : = x.

Transform conflicting interests into parallel interests
At the heart of economics lies the transformation of conflicts about the distribution of scarcity into parallel interests regarding the alleviation of want. In this way, people become partners in creating value instead of being adversaries. The discipline of economics helps convert the downward spiral of poverty and conflict into the upward spiral of wellbeing and peace.

Finance as relational infrastructure to trade time...
Financial markets and institutions constitute a key part of the relational infrastructure of our society, which allows people to trade across time and across contingencies. As regards time, entrepreneurs with excellent ideas for innovation typically have neither the money nor the risk capacity to finance innovation. Others who own capital and have greater risk appetite, yet lack innovative ideas, can finance these entrepreneurs. In this way, both the financiers and the innovators benefit; the innovators

can implement their ideas, while the financiers enjoy a good return on their savings. The capacity of financial markets to diversify risks by spreading these risks across many individuals makes risky investments with high social returns feasible. Financial markets thus reconcile growth and solidarity.

…and risks

Indeed, financial markets and institutions implement solidarity. In particular, financial institutions allow people to pool idiosyncratic risks. As regards systematic risks, financial markets allow these risks to be shifted to those agents who can best bear risks. In this case, too, all parties benefit: risk-averse individuals get rid of risks while risk-takes benefit from associated risk premiums.

4. Finance out of balance

Human rationality and morality…

With our intellect, consciousness and morality, we can establish relationships between our choices, on the one hand, and the short-term and long-term consequences for ourselves and others on the other. The ability to look beyond our immediate emotions has allowed humanity to conquer the world.

…is limited

And yet we should not be naïve: the capacity of humans to relate their actions to consequences is limited. In the language of economics, people feature bounded rationality as well as bounded morality. Bounded rationality limits people in their ability to make sensible choices (Kahneman, 2011). Bounded morality can frustrate good cooperation. In particular, people can harm each other if they think they may profit from doing so. They also feature limited empathy for others; the ability to look beyond our own immediate interests is bounded. Limits to rationality and morality are related: people tend to overestimate the moral quality of their own decisions, while understating the moral motivations of others (Ariely, 2012).

Unbalanced choices destroy value

The limits of rationality and morality result in unbalanced choices. Money illusion – excessive love of money – is an illustration. Due to our limited morality, others do not always trust us. Instead, they suspect that we will damage their interests. Hence, they refrain from cooperating with us. Fear of greed thus destroys value.

Governance problems in finance: 'phishing for phools'...

Finance constitutes not only an opportunity (see section 3) but also a threat to human flourishing. Just like the health care and education sectors, finance faces serious governance problems because of bounded rationality and bounded morality. As regards limited rationality, many consumers are financially illiterate. In fact, various behavioural biases cause consumers to make systematic mistakes when trading time and risks. Opportunistic traders can take advantage of these biases in order to benefit themselves: they 'phish for phools' (Akerlof and Shiller, 2015). In competitive markets, the best deceivers survive, rather than those suppliers who best serve consumers. The financial sector may thus become a den of thieves rather than a valuable infrastructure for implementing solidarity.

... contagious systematic risks...

Another problem facing financial markets is that their fragility may lead to macroeconomic instability. In the face of fundamental uncertainty, boundedly rational people look at others to form expectations and to find out what is valuable. As a consequence of conformist behaviour, the financial sector can put a multiplier on human judgment biases. 'Groupthink' makes the economy fragile; fear and euphoria are contagious. Small shocks can result in large, systematic risks. Whereas financial markets may thus help protect people against risks, they may also foster new risks by creating bubbles. Indeed, the value of financial assets is determined to a large extent by their resale value, rather than by objective fundamental qualities. To ascertain the value of an asset, we thus have to induce the subjective values others attach to it. Its value is socially constructed through what Milton Keynes referred to as 'beauty contests.'

…and unintended effects of public policy
Government policies aimed at alleviating these market failures can have the unintended effect of exacerbating them. To illustrate, providing guarantees to prevent panic in economically bad times can result in excessive risk taking during good times. The moral hazard associated with these behavioural effects causes public trust to deteriorate rather than raising macroeconomic stability.

5. Finance in more balance

Institutions as limitations on behaviour
The third and final step in the narrative of hope is to create more balance through better institutions. These institutions form the traffic rules that prevent people from hurting themselves or others. Institutions discipline people to protect vulnerable goals or interests. The three main modes of governance are coercion, freedom, and voluntary commitment. They are related to the institutions of, respectively, government, market, and identity.

Coercion
Coercion makes the strong party weaker. By thus protecting the weak party and disciplining the strong party to account for the interests of the weak party, compulsion of the stronger party may enhance trust in the balance of win-win. This may result in more value-enhancing cooperation. The government can employ coercion. The disadvantage of coercion is that leaders may lack morality or rationality: they may abuse their power or they may lack relevant information. Coercion can also harm the intrinsic motivation of those who are subject to it.

Competition
The second governance mechanism – competition – makes the weaker party stronger. The threat of exchangeability stimulates strong parties to take account of the interests of others in order to protect their reputation as a reliable and trustworthy partner. Competition can only work well if information about effort is public and participants in the market share a

common understanding about the responsibilities of all.

Voluntary commitment: self-regulation
Voluntary commitment takes an intermediary position between coercion and free exchangeability. With this governance method of self-regulation, people are intrinsically motivated to serve the interests of the weak party because they wish to protect the relationship. Being part of a bigger whole gives their lives meaning and purpose. People are intrinsically motivated to serve others and protect their identity as part of a larger, meaningful whole (Ariely, 2012). Leaders can build common identities. A disadvantage of this way of governing is that empathy may become unbalanced; bonding may occur at the expense of outsiders (Green, 2013). Moreover, leaders may build identities to reap personal benefit at the expense of others.

Governance remains imperfect
All three main governance mechanisms face limitations and feature side effects. Hence, combining the three forms of governance is often best. Dilemmas also remain. For example, an important trade-off that takes place is between regulation and liberalism: preventing win-lose but providing enough freedom and flexibility to allow sufficient scope for win-win. In the end, governance will always remain imperfect.

Regulation and debt as coercion: strengths…
In the financial sector, coercion appears in the form of government regulation. Debt contracts can also be classified under coercion. Debt contracts are complete contracts that are enforced through the courts. These courts protect the weak party: for example, the creditor who must trust the debtor to return the borrowed money.

…and weaknesses…
Unfortunately, debt also suffers from inherent weaknesses. First of all, risk sharing tends to be inefficient. In particular, the debtor bears risks that he has no control over. Even if the financed project does not yield any return, the debtor still has to pay the creditor. Due to this inefficient

risk sharing, a risk-averse debtor may decide not to invest in a project even if it is a socially valuable. Another disadvantage of government regulation or contracts that prescribe the behaviour of the debtor is that they may crowd out intrinsic motivation. A complete contract enforced by a third party indicates a lack of trust, which then becomes a self-ful-filling prophecy.

...because of distorted incentives for risk taking
A final drawback of debt contracts is that they may distort a debtor's risk-taking incentives. Especially if the debtor is close to bankruptcy or already carries substantial debt, he has an incentive to take excessive risks. This is because he benefits from the upside of borrowing money, but can shift the downsides to the creditor. Indeed, with little equity financing, creditors in effect provide a put option to the owners who benefit from limited liability. Public guarantees can exacerbate these risk-taking incentives because any downward risk can be shifted to the government. Incentives for creditors to police debtors are thus eroded. Such incentives for excessive risk-taking contribute to macroeconomic instability by worsening debt overhang problems in economically bad times.

Liquidity and competition: Strengths...
Another way to govern financial cooperation is liquidity: people can trade their financial relationship with others. Exchangeability and the associated competition discipline those who demand capital to take into account the interests of the providers of capital. If they fail to do so, suppliers of capital will sell their claims. This lowers the price of claims issued so that it becomes more expensive for those who demand new capital to raise it.

...and weaknesses...
Competition and the associated liquidity of exchangeability also suffer from serious problems. Lack of public information about those seeking capital can cause the reputational mechanism to fail. Asymmetric information may result in adverse selection, thereby limiting the tradability of the claims. This may result in herd behaviour and the associated risk of

fragility. Indeed, in economically bad times, liquidity may vanish when confidence suddenly dries up due to blind panic. Imperfect information may also lead to moral hazard; the associated fear of the capital suppliers that the capital-seeking party holds them up blocks mutually advantageous cooperation.

…because of transactional perspective

Just like coercion, liquidity may crowd out intrinsic motivation. Exchangeability is not very motivating because it may signal a lack of trust. Indeed, people attach intrinsic value to the quality of a relationship as signalled by the commitment of all parties to it. In this case, too, a lack of trust may become self-fulfilling. Finally, liquidity implies a transactional rather than a relational perspective. This short-term perspective may discourage specific investments in knowing, trusting and appreciating others. A lack of specific investments in valuable relationships may destroy value.

More transactional debt because of more relational equity finance

One way to improve governance in the financial sector is to make finance less complicated and opaque. Improved public information alleviates the market failures associated with asymmetric information. To reduce the opportunities for theft and deceit in the financial sector, more equity finance is called for in banks and other corporations. With more equity finance in both financial and non-financial corporations, debt becomes a less complicated contract. With more relational equity finance, debt becomes more transactional. In particular, if banks carry more equity finance, they face fewer incentives to take excessive risks and burden the public purse. As a direct consequence, less regulation is needed and banks can be entrusted with more discretion. In fact, with tax payers becoming less important stakeholders, banks become more private institutions.

6. More relational finance

Relationships versus transactions

Equity finance is typically more relational and thus less liquid than debt finance. To enhance the quality of governance in the financial sector, we must move to more durable relationships based on incomplete agreements ('equity') rather than to short-term transactions and/or complete contracts ('debt'). This is in effect the third way of governance that comes in-between coercion ('complete contracts'), on the one hand, and exchangeability ('liquidity'), on the other. These relationships are based on tacit agreements ('equity' or (in Dutch) 'eigen vermogen') rather than on explicitly codified legal contracts ('debt' or (in Dutch) 'vreemd vermogen'). Indeed, the enforcement of these implicit agreements relies more on mutual trust and a common identity and less on the courts.

Relational governance in a complex, dynamic world

An advantage of this 'relational' mode of governance compared to the 'transactional mode' of complete contracts is that it can be based on private information and does not have to rely on public and verifiable information only. Moreover, it does not have to rely on agreements that are explicitly codified in advance but can be based on shared implicit understandings. Hence, these 'equity' types of agreements can deal better with unexpected contingencies. They therefore tend to result in more efficient risk sharing. Indeed, creditors rather than debtors may bear risks that neither party can influence, because the parties know the origin of risks and trust that people do not shift risks onto others. This relational type of governance seems suited for more dynamic, complex cooperation. This explains why firms and clients in many industries form more durable relationships in a modern economy.

Specific investments in knowing, trusting and appreciating each other

Compared to liquidity and exchangeability, voluntary commitment implies better incentives for specific investments in getting to know each other and building up mutual trust, empathy, appreciation and a common 'we' identity. Parties see their short-term sacrifices in the context of the long-term benefits from the relationship: they have a shared past and future. Moreover, gift exchange in the form of exchanging trust and service may contribute to the quality of the relationship, which people intrinsically value. Indeed, humans intrinsically value reciprocal relationships in which they are trusted and valued and in which they are not exchangeable for another party. Being of real significance to the other party gives their life meaning and provides intrinsic motivation to serve the other's interest. A relationship in which parties trust and value each other and are mutually dependent on one another thus contributes directly to welfare – irrespective of the exchanged goods and services. Relationships are not only means but also goals in their own right.

Drawbacks of relationships
Relationships also suffer from disadvantages. In equity finance, those seeking capital typically enjoy less privacy and autonomy (and sovereignty) than in debt finance. Creditors will want to know them better and may jointly govern the relationship. Indeed, 'voice' rather than 'exit' is a more important governance mode in relational forms of finance than in debt finance. The capital suppliers are less flexible to leave the relationship if unexpected shocks occur. In other words, they are less liquid.[1] This means that just like debtors, they have less control and sovereignty over an aspect of their lives because of their commitment to the relationship. They are also more exposed to the credit risk of the counterparty, e.g. because of the counterparty not serving the mutual interest (i.e. moral hazard) or because of adverse shocks that the counterparty cannot influence (i.e. solidarity). Creditors cannot easily diversify their claim over various debtors because of scale economies in getting to know their partners: they face a trade-off between superficial cooperation with many stakeholders and intensive cooperation with only a few. Compared to transactions, they are thus more vulnerable in relationships: not only to liquidity risk but also to credit (or counterparty) risk. In relationships, cooperation is limited to a few partners to which one is committed. This constrains mutually advantageous cooperation.

Distorted choice between flexibility and voluntary commitment...
Various factors distort the balance between the liquidity and flexibility of transactions and the voluntary commitment of relationships. First of all, taxes favour debt over equity. Second, various government guarantees implicitly subsidise liquidity transformation by banks over disinter-mediated financial relationships. Third, people tend to underestimate their ability to absorb shocks due to myopic loss aversion. They fail to adequately project changes in the so-called 'reference point' and are thus excessively risk averse. Indeed, their negative emotional responses to adverse shocks are much more short-lived than people anticipate.

... calls for debt-equity swaps
To alleviate the bias towards complete debt contracts and the liquidity of transactions, the tax privileges of debt finance should be reduced. Moreover, to cut the implicit subsidies to debt finance, capital require-ments of banks should be raised. Furthermore, financiers should be bailed-in when capital requirements are inadequate – this means that they become explicitly risk-bearing. Other debt-equity swaps are also called for, all with the goal of making finance more relational.

7. Conclusions

Balance in models of human behaviour
By teaching a richer variety of models of human behaviour, we can restore the balance between the model of the self-interested hawk of the *homo economicus* and the model of the naïve dove who also cares about others. On the one hand, we should be realistic about the capacity of humans to hurt others. On the other hand, we should also be aware of the potential of humans to cooperate and grow in the type of virtuous behaviour that protects the interests of others.

A balanced view on finance as opportunity and threat
The financial sector is a potential source of both blessing (section 3) and curse (section 4). Whereas financial markets may help protect people against risks, they may also create new risks. Indeed, bounded rationality

and morality yield serious governance problems in the financial sector. The limited rationality of consumers makes it essential for suppliers to be willing to take account of the interests of consumers. The limited morality of suppliers, however, makes such trust problematic.

Hope as a narrow road between naivety and cynicism
The economics of hope outlined in this paper is the third, narrow road between the broad roads of naivety and cynicism. It seeks to avoid both utopianism and scepticism. The road of naïve utopianism and optimism denies the darkness of evil. As such, it is essentially false hope: opium for the people. The road of cynicism, in contrast, argues that the world is worthless and hopeless.

Cooperation involves risk by transferring control…
We should not be naïve about the risks of cooperation and relationships in general. Cooperation demands not only transferring sovereignty and control, but also the exercise of courage to accept the vulnerability of credit and illiquidity risk. It also requires the ability to learn and forgive (Bruni 2012). The uncertainty surrounding relationships is the direct consequence of the freedom of humans whose rationality and morality are limited.

… in finance, like anywhere else
Human cooperation – in finance and elsewhere – involves taking risks and accepting uncertainty. Rather than protecting themselves against all mishaps through control over others, parties are called to be vulnerable by giving others the freedom to fail (Bruni 2012). They dare to trust people even though their counterparties feature limited rationality and limited morality.

…through more relational forms of finance
Transforming the tendency to control others through complete legal contracts requires a cultural transformation. The same holds for the tendency to protect ourselves against risk by making others exchangeable through liquid financial instruments. In this connection, more relational

forms of finance than liquid debt are called for. Ex ante, this requires the courage to extend the credit of trust and thus take on credit risk. This shows respect for others and gives partners the opportunity to give their lives meaning. Ex post, it demands the resilience to deal with mishaps and unexpected shocks. Responding to adverse shocks with the hopeful light of forgiveness and hope instead of blame is one of the best antibodies available to combat the epidemic of fear, greed, and indifference.

1. The liquidity transformation of banks can reconcile liquidity with earning the illiquidity premium. This, however, results in potential instability and governance problems, and requires extensive regulation by the government or other stakeholders.

Bibliography

Akerlof, G.A., and R. Kranton. *Identity Economics: How Our Identities Shape Our Work, Wages, and Well-Being.* Princeton: University Press, 2010.

Akerlof, G. A., and R. J. Shiller. *Animal Spirits: How Human Psychology Drives the Economy, and Why It Matters for Global Capitalism.* Princeton: University Press, 2009.

Akerlof, G. A., and R. J. Shiller. *Phishing for Phools. The Economics of Manipulation and Deception.* Princeton: University Press, 2015.

Ariely, D. *The (Honest) Truth about Dishonesty.* New York: Harper Collins, 2012.

Bovenberg, A. L. 'Economieonderwijs in Balans: Kiezen en Samenwerken.' Inaugural Lecture, Tilburg University, 15 Dec. 2016, Tilburg.

Bruni, L. *The Wound and the Blessing. Economics, Relationships, and Happiness.* New York: New City Press, 2012.

Bowles, S. *Moral Economy. Why Good Incentives Are No Substitute for Good Citizens.* New Haven: Yale University Press, 2016.

Grant, A. 'Does Studying Economics Breed Greed?' *Psychology Today,* 22 Oct. 2013.

Greene, J. *Moral Tribes. Emotion, Reason, and the Gap Between Us and Them.* London: Atlantic Books, 2013.

Heckman, J. 'Policies to Foster Human Capital.' *Research in Economics* 54 (2000): 3-56.

Kahneman, D. *Thinking, Fast and Slow.* New York: Farrar, Straus and Giroux, 2011.

Keynes, J. *The General Theory of Employment, Interest and Money.* Basingstoke: Palgrave Macmillan, 2007.

Keynes, J. *Letter to Roy Harrod.* July 4, 1938.

Ostrom, E. 'Beyond Markets and States: Polycentric Governance of Complex Economic Systems.' *American Economic Review* 100 (2009): 641-672.

Sachs, J. 'Investing in Social Capital.' In *World Happiness Report 2015,* eds. J.F. Helliwell, R. Layard and J. Sachs. New York: United Nations, 2015.

Smith, A. *Wealth of Nations.* Bks. I, II, and XXVI. London: Methuen & Co, 1776.

Van Winden, F. 'Political Economy at a Crossroads, On the Role of Emotions and Relationships towards a Decision Science.' Valedictory lecture, University of Amsterdam, 3 June 2016, Amsterdam.

Wilkinson, N., and M. Klaes. *An Introduction to Behavioural Economics.* New York: Palgrave Macmillan, 2012.

It's all about us

By Cor van Beuningen and Kees Buitendijk

1. Introduction

IN HIS CONTRIBUTION to the present volume, former Minister of Finance of the Netherlands Wouter Bos recalls the public outrage that he caused back in 2008. When asked by the presenter of a popular talk show who was to blame for the crisis, he simply answered: 'we are'. How did Bos dare blame us, noble citizens, instead of bankers? Quoting Goethe and Robert Reich, Bos explains that we all carry more than one soul in our chest. We are citizens, but we are also consumers, investors, and money savers. In each situation, our goals and intentions are different; but when it comes down to it, the soul that argues for morality loses from other souls arguing for returns, profits, and low prices. Bos says: "[T]his is one of the lessons I learned from the crisis: the causes of it go deep into the veins of our society, our economic behaviours and our morality." And he wonders: "Can we avoid another crisis? Can we change?"

In this contribution, we will further explore the souls of the twenty-first century (wo-)man and the possibilities for change. Above all, we ask if the eventuality of another financial crisis is really our main problem.

2. The Entrepreneurial Self

"This is about who we are today, and how we have become who we are. It is about the engineers of the modern soul."
– Professor Peter Miller, London School of Economics & Political Science,
reviewing Ulrich Bröckling, The Entrepreneurial Self

In his widely acclaimed *Das unternehmerische Selbst - Soziologie einer Subjektivierungsform* (2007; English trans. *The Entrepreneurial Self: Fabricating a New Type of Subject*, London 2016), Ulrich Bröckling traces the emergence of the "entrepreneurial self" in the mid-seventies of last century, concomitant with the restructuring process of the social welfare state and the ascendance of neoliberalism. The entrepreneurial self (or

TES) is an interpellation to act, in all spheres of life, the way an entrepreneur does when conducting business. For Bröckling, TES is a form of *subjectification*:

> An entrepreneur is something we are supposed to become. The call to act as an entrepreneur of one's own life produces a model for people to understand what they are and what they ought to be, and it tells them how to work on the self in order to become what they ought to be. [..] It is an *aim* individuals strife for, a *gauge* by which they judge their own conduct, a daily *exercise* for working on the self, and finally a *truth generator* by which they come to know themselves. (2015, Foreword).

As an entrepreneur, one should be constantly excited and ready for action. Life is about calculating profits and losses, being highly creative, approaching others as clients (or competitors), being willing to solve problems, to make tireless and renewed attempts to achieve success, and to remain resilient to adversity (Stachowiak 2018).

The entrepreneurial self is moulded on the market, presenting self-realization and economic success both as desire and duty (Bröckling 2015, p 202). Here, the market is to be conceived as the most efficient as well as the *just* mechanism for the allocation of success and failure; and competition is to be conceived as the essence and the main virtue of capitalist markets.

For Bröckling, it is clear that markets nor competition come about naturally, but that they must be actively instituted and sustained: "If the thrust of neoliberal government is toward generalising competition, modelling society as a whole on the market, then it will ineluctably come to mould subjectivity on the figure of the entrepreneur" (in Overwijk 2018, p.60)

In the neoliberal world, in which society is organized like a company, modelling one's own actions to mirror those of an entrepreneur is the quickest way to attain social recognition. Indeed, acting entrepreneurially is the very condition for participating in modern social life: "Moved by the desire to stay in touch and the fear of dropping out of the society of competition, people answer the call to be entrepreneurial by helping to create the very reality it already presupposed." (Bröckling 2015).

Thus, for Bröckling, the entrepreneurial self is a 'Realfiktion', i.e. a fictive idea that once evoked is made reality by those who are addressed: *Sie schaffen dadurch jene Wirklichkeit mit, welche die unternehmerische Anrufung immer schon als gegeben unterstellt* (Bröckling, 2008). This fiction has proven to be very effective when it comes to mobilizing people, generating commitment, and instilling desire. By the turn of the century, the entrepreneurial self had become the hegemonic soul (Bührmann 2005), replacing both Organisational Man and the egalitarian Client of the Welfare State of the previous periods.

3. TES as institutional logic

TES posits economic success and market value both as duty and desire. More precisely, it envisions these as the purpose and meaning of both being (what we are - to become) and doing. The entrepreneurial self is effectively inscribed in the soul of twenty-first century man, constituting – and in turn being constituted by – the society as a marketplace; to this extent, TES can best be conceived as a generalized institutional logic, i.e. as a grammar of meaningful practice that binds subjects, practices, and objects in persistent constellations that afford and draw upon particular affects and effects (Friedland 2018).

It should be noted that TES is not a mere ideological imposition that works on authority and control. As Konings forcefully observes, the traditional critique of capitalism as "a cold monster that imposes a regime of depersonalised calculation and an abstract utilitarian rationality" (2015) (REF) falls short. TES cannot be understood without taking seriously the centrality of emotions and affect. In Konings' own words, one must ascribe to the central importance of belief, sentiment, and faith (2015). Recall Robert Pirsig: "The passions, the emotions, the affective domain of man's consciousness, […] are the central part of nature's order" (2006, p.287).

Note 1. Jonathan Haidt highlights this importance with a pointed metaphor: "Man is an emotional dog with a rational tail; anytime body and tail disagree about which direction to go, the tail is going to lose". This is to say that affects (feelings and intuitions) and emotions are the basic drivers of behaviour, eventually adjusted by rational deliberation (cf. Daniel Kahneman's 'dual system' as described in his book Thinking, Fast and Slow (2011) system 1 is fast, instinctive, and emotional, while system 2 is slower, more deliberative, and more logical). Affects and emotions involve complex psycho-physiological (i.e. embodied) processes (Haidt 2001)). Affect theory is originally attributed to Silvan Tomkins, who stressed the biological nature of affects. He distinguished nine biologically based affects: joy, interest/excitement, surprise, shame, distress, fear, anger, dissmell (or distaste), and contempt/disgust. Later, Hugo Lövheim elaborated the famous cube of emotions, a model in which he proposes a direct relation between specific combinations of the high/low levels of three neurotransmitters (serotonin - the happiness hormone, dopamine - the reward hormone, and noradrenaline - the staying-focused hormone) with these affects or basic emotions.

Affective states vary along three principal dimensions: valence, arousal, and motivational intensity. Valence is the like-dislike evaluation of an experienced state. Arousal, varying from calm to agitated, is closely related to motivational intensity, but they differ in that motivation necessarily implies action while arousal does not. Like affects, emotions – such as gratitude, pity, jealousy, grief, awe, and sadness - are perceptual and embodied, but emotions are culturally informed and more complex mental states. Emotions are not only individual reactions but also intersubjective, collective experiences; both in a bodily and also in an inherently social sense, since they are experienced in a world of relations connecting human beings to each other and the world around them.

With regard to TES, emotions are involved, *first and foremost*, in the way it engages and commits people to economic success and market value as prized ends, and to market and competition as just and virtuous mechanisms. In answering the interpellation and putting it in practice, people invest emotionally in the prized ends and values, which in turn generates the necessary energies to put TES to work and make it come true.

Second, emotions are involved in actual entrepreneurial practice, both in our day-to-day desire for the prized ends as well as in the efforts deployed (*telos* and *ethos*), and again in the emotions that are afforded by the doing itself. Emotions not only encourage us to work; they are part of the work, part of what makes that work *work* (Friedland, 2017-2) and what makes us keep on working. Friedland argues that "[w]e cleave to institutional ways of doing because of the way they make us feel; indeed we are the way they make us feel. Institutions are not only ways of doing, but of being" (2017-1).

Third, TES not only instils a desire, but also a duty, i.e. the moral obligation to make use of the freedom to deploy and develop one's assets and compete for the prized ends of success and market value. Indeed, deploying successfully one's qualities generates a gratifying feeling of freedom – in fact *this is* freedom, if we subscribe to the definition of Frithjof Bergmann in *On Freedom*. For Bergman, an act is free if the actor identifies with the elements from which it flows: "Freedom [...] is the expression of what we are, of the qualities and characteristics we possess, but in an unpretentious sense; it is the expression of qualities with which we identify" (in Kamber 1978).

Naturally, the flipside of this is that freedom comes with responsibility – for instance, for one's losses and failures in the marketplace. This is how, according to Kotsko, we are all "bedeviled" by neoliberalism. He argues:

> "The market chooses winners and losers, and we all choose how to equip ourselves for market competition. Whatever happens, no matter how apparently unjust or arbitrary, thus reflects the free choice of everyone involved, which is in turn reflected in market outcomes. [...] The neoliberal concept of freedom [..] not only is limited to market transactions; it is also limited to generating blameworthiness, [...] to tell us that we deserve what we get." (2018-2)

Following Phillip Petit, one might say that TES offers ample agency-freedom and little option-freedom. Option freedom refers to the amount of choice available; agency freedom is fixed in a more complex way by the recognized status of the agent in relation to his or her fellows (2003). TES might then be considered an example of agency freedom without option freedom – but with freedom nonetheless.

TES connects the self and society. The entrepreneurial self both defines and shapes the outside world according to its principles, i.e. as a marketplace full of opportunities, clients, and competitors. Again, it shapes *the very reality it already presupposed* (Bröckling 2015). Both subject (the entrepreneurial self) and object (the outside world as a marketplace) are emergent, that is becoming; and in their evolving relationship they co-constitute each other. Bröcklings *Realfiktion* not only generates the self (or soul) that it evokes, it also "produces" the corresponding practices, relationships, and objects, i.e. the marketised society which in turn shapes the self. In this sense, subjectification and objectification, or psychogenesis and sociogenesis, go hand in hand (as Norbert Elias already noted back in 1939 in his *Über den Prozeß der Zivilisation. Soziogenetische und psychogenetische Untersuchungen*; cf. Mennell).

This would explain the success and resilience of TES as institutional logic: it is the very system that works to make resistance or change almost impossible or unimaginable. The failure of the entrepreneurial self to realise its promise does not necessarily detract from its engagement. In fact, as Konings notes, these failures have an uncanny way of intensifying our attachment to it. In a way, its modus operandi is similar to what Wendy Brown has described as "wounded attachments", attachments which serve to intensify our faith in the very structure of connections that are letting us down (in Allon 2015).

4. The entrepreneurial self's progeny

In a foreword to the English edition of his work (published 2015), Bröckling considers that TES has confirmed its own conceptual validity. In fact, the crisis has increased the pressure to develop individual distinctions in order to stay competitive. At the same time, he writes, a new figure has to be added to that of the entrepreneurial self: *the indebted man,* which might be conceived as a subspecies, with its own peculiarities. Bröckling notes: "While the entrepreneurial self is continually concerned with sniffing out profit opportunities, the indebted self must perpetually re-establish its credit rating [..] and, over and over again, open up its books, and make a convincing show of being able to pay back its credit. The entrepreneurial self is never finished with self-optimizing, the indebted self can never retire from self-revelation." Here, Bröckling is referring to recent research done on this subject – debt in relation to the self – by among others Lazzarato and Feher.

In *The Making of the Indebted Man* (2012), Mauricio Lazzarato takes the paradigmatic case of American students, who graduate with ever-rising amounts of debts. Students enter the labour market as an adult paying off a seemingly endless series of debts: credit cards, students loans, then on to mortgages, and so on and so forth. According to Lazzarato,

> debt is the technique most adequate to the production of neoliberalism's *homo economicus*. Students not only consider themselves human capital, which they must valorise through their own investments (the university loans they take out) but also feel compelled to act, think, and behave as if they were individual businesses. Debt requires an apprenticeship in certain behavior, accounting rules, and organizational principles, traditionally implemented within a corporation, [for] people who have not yet gone on the job market. [...] Students' debt mortgages at once their behavior, wages, and future income. Credit produces a specific form of subjectification. (in Gratton 2015)

Debt creates a constraining "memory of the future", endowing the debtor "with interiority, a conscience", and "neutralizing time as the creation of new possibilities" (Kloeckner 2018).

In *Rated Agency: Investee Politics in a Speculative Age*, Michael Feher elaborates on the other side of debt, i.e. credit, and the need for the entrepreneurial self to maintain and increase its creditworthiness, that is, its rating. Feher contends that, while the original entrepreneurial self was driven to act and think like an entrepreneur (that is, to make decisions based on cost/benefit calculations and the optimization of profit), the actual outcome of TES is that individuals are encouraged to act and think like an asset manager or *investee*. TES now has to care about its attractiveness in the eyes of the investor. This shift is linked to the transition from a commercial, profit-based economy operated through trading markets, to a reputational, credit-based economy (2016).

The *investee condition* applies to both publicly traded firms, states, and individuals. With regard to the first, corporate governance does not aim anymore "to maximize the difference between sales revenues and production costs over the long term. Its sole objective is eliciting an increase, in the very near future, of the value assigned by financial markets to the stock held by shareholders" (Feher 2019). On example of the effect of this is that buying back shares of one's own company is now considered a sound practice, with a view to attracting investors whose sole concern is the shareholder value of the firms they finance.

Similarly, states will go a long way in order to maintain and increase their ratings in the bond markets and thus please bondholders by catering to their preferences, e.g. through financial deregulation, the lowering of corporate taxes, flexibilisation of labour, and the cutting of social programmes (Feher 2019-1).

Finally, the pursuit of creditworthiness also informs the conduct of the individual entrepreneurial self. It is now up to "free agents", "freelancers", "private contractors", and job applicants to increase and showcase their assets. Assets are both sources of income and collaterals that enable the credit-seeking asset manager to borrow. Feher mentions that "[s]ome showcase highly prized skills and an appealing social network, while others are left to present their unlimited availability and flexibility as attractive assets" (2019-2).

Like the entrepreneurial self, the self as *the rated agency* or *the invested self* (TIS) is a form of subjectification that is part and parcel of an institutional logic. While TES is an interpellation to act as an entre-preneur in the marketplace, TIS is an interpellation to act as the manager of one's own portfolio, with a view to seeking credit / investment in the financial marketplace and opening up one's investments to the judgments of investors, with the promise of (self-esteem generated by) investments that come from creditors, employers, and so on (Bowser 2015).

TIS can be seen as TES' progeny and is inscribed in the soul of the twenty-first century citizen. With regard to this, Ganz complains that the rated agency is "an incursion of the metabolic process of economy into our very souls" (2019) (REF), invoking the dystopian future represented by the system of societal credit being implemented in China, which turns citizens into social pariahs if they fall under a certain rating.

For Feher, these shifts are integral to the process of *financialisa-tion*. This concept requires some clarification, as it can be understood in a number of ways. In fact, different definitions tend to highlight different aspects of the process as a whole. For instance, 'financialisation' can refer to the increasing relative size of the financial sector in the GDP of developed economies; to the volume of profits made by financial companies compared with those of other enterprises; and to the proportion of portfolio income — relative to commercial cash flow — in the accounts of nonfinancial firms (Feher 2019-1). In his contribution to the present volume, Bezemer uses the term to denote "the application of the logic of finance to domains where it does not belong: where cost/benefit analyses, the tracking of virtual and fluctuating wealth, or the use of financial stimuli are harmful rather than beneficial. For this reason, we must consider the ubiquity of 'the financial', which we have come to understand in the concept of 'financialisation'" (REF). With this definition, Bezemer points to the fact that the institutional logic of financialisation has been spreading to ever more domains of social life. Alternatively, for Krippner, financialisation refers to "a pattern of accumulation in which profits accrue primarily through financial channels rather than through trade and commodity production" (2005, p.174). Meanwhile, according to Feher, "over and above such indicators — the examination of which corroborates the thesis of a massive transfer of funds from the "real economy" to speculative financial circuits — what truly manifests the ascendancy of credit suppliers is their ability to select the projects that deserve to be financed" (2019-1); in other words, the hegemony of finance.

The invested self – or maybe more appropriately: *the financialised self* (TFS) – adopts the viewpoint of the credit supplier or investor and their requirements. To the extent that all spheres of social life, of society, are effectively financialised, it is finance – ultimately, the owners of capital – that decides what will exist and what will disappear. Furthermore, it dictates *how* something will exist, since financialised logics and practices reshape all performance metrics.

5. Can we change course / ourselves?

We started this exposé with the questions raised by Wouter Bos: can we avoid another crisis? Can we change, and tame that greedy soul in our chest? Our exploration of the soul of the twenty-first century (wo-)man yielded two selves (or maybe one and a subspecies): the entrepreneurial self, or TES, and the financialised self, or TFS. As generalized institutional logics, TES and TFS constitute – and in turn are constituted by – the society as a (financial) marketplace. They shape a self and a society that co-constitute each other. Both selves are moulded on the market, presenting self-realisation (chiefly agency and freedom) and profit/creditworthiness as both desire and duty. They both derive their strength and success from the fact that they are able to command loyalty and engagement of the self. They do so by drawing upon and affording particular effects and affects, or emotions (cf. Konings' belief, sentiment, and faith).

With an eye to the distinct possibility of another financial crisis, all this does not bode well. And yet a new financial crisis should not be our biggest concern. Perhaps that crisis is no more than a periodically occurring surface expression (along with many others – cf.. Stiglitz 2019-2) of a long-term underground peat fire that consumes the foundations of human flourishing and peaceful society.

Confronted by this state of affairs, moral indignation (such as anger for *"greedy" practices*) is both useless and out of place, because it fails to understand the underlying systemic logic of subjectification that "bedevils" or "alienates" all.. Michael Heinrich refers to this as the *Verblendungszusammenhang* that affects us all, making moral criticism of our behaviour pointless (Heinrich).

In a similar vein, it seems pointless to expect – as Stiglitz does - change coming from above, i.e. from politics and the state. As long as TES and TFS effectively shape both our selves and our society, no electoral majorities will be found for radical change. Moreover, the state itself is deeply enmeshed in financialised logic: its manoeuvring space is severely limited both by the need to maintain its rating in the bond market and by international competition (Stiglitz 2019-2).

This can only lead to a single conclusion. There is no escape and no other cure; it's about us.

Change is possible, but Stiglitz is right when he writes that "there is no magic bullet that can reverse the damage done by decades of neoliberalism" (Stiglitz 2019-2). Let us indicate the steps to take on the road to undoing that damage.

The first thing is to understand the modus operandi of both TES and TFS as strong and resilient self- and society shaping institutional logics, and particularly their capacity to command loyalty by affording embodied affects and emotions.

Following this, we must recognize that institutional logic – *any* institutional logic – may indeed bedevil us, narrowing and distorting our view, enchanting us, and alienating us. An institutional logic can indeed be conceived as a *Verblendunszusammenhang*, a persistent constellation that blinds us, even "takes us out of ourselves, offering perpetual possibility and the constitutive risks of *ekstasis*" (Friedland 2018). The prized ends – status, profit, creditworthiness – may become objects of idolatry; meanwhile, the feelings they evoke and the passions involved may well become addictive. Along the way, both *telos* and *ethos* are disfigured.

The following step consists of a pause, in order to get rid of our entanglement and look at the effects of this institutional logic. We must ask ourselves: what is it doing to/with me, others, and the world? Finally, we must ask ourselves if this is what we want – for us, for others, and for the world. If the answer is negative, then we must free ourselves from the system's logic and organizes ourselves and our work in more humanising arrangements. Philosopher Paul van Tongeren and economist Lans Bovenberg may help us on the way.

Paul van Tongeren wrote a beautiful essay on human flourishing, or in fact about being / becoming human. He argues: "People are not what they are before they enter into relationships of recognition and care. A person becomes a person by the way in which and the extent to which he is recognized and loved as a person. And that recognition and that love are not given separately, but in all the ways in which people relate to each other" (2001)

In all the ways in which people relate to each other. Just imagine the relation between an investor and an entrepreneur; how can this be made into a vehicle for humanizing interaction?

Van Tongeren takes the case of the relation between teacher and pupil, the functional core of which is a transfer of knowledge. And yet: "The dedication of a teacher to the student not only makes his teaching more effective; it also forms the student into a person in his/her own right". This works both ways: "The teacher not only earns money through the lessons he gives, but also becomes a person to the extent in which he is recognized as a person by the student - or he is mutilated because that recognition does not take place." As such, a functional interface is made into a relationship of mutual recognition and care. If we succeed in achieving this recognition, we receive a bonus: our education, i.e. the functional core of the relationship, is more effective.

We return to our earlier question: can we turn the interface between an investor and an entrepreneur into a vehicle for humanizing interaction, instead of it being governed by the systemic logic of the financial marketplace? And along the way, might we acquire bonus of heightened effectiveness?

Fortunately, we may refer to the contribution of Lans Bovenberg in the present volume, which constitutes a plea for relational rather than transactional modes of governance in finance and for a shift away from liquidity and debt finance to equity. Bovenberg concludes: "Ex ante, this requires the courage to extend the credit of trust and thus take on credit risk. This shows respect for others and gives partners the opportunity to give their lives meaning. Ex post, it demands the resilience to deal with mishaps and unexpected shocks. Responding to adverse shocks with the hopeful light of forgiveness and hope instead of blame is one of the best antibodies available to combat the epidemic of fear, greed, and indifference". We could not have told it better.

Bibliography

Allon, Fiona (2015): On capitalism emotional logics. Available from: http://ppesydney.net/on-capitalisms-emotional-logics/

Bowser, Josh (2015): Another Speculation? Michel Feher on Neoliberalism and Resistance.
Available from: http://blogs.nottingham.ac.uk/criticalmoment/2015/07/22/another-speculation-michel-feher-on-neoliberalism-and-resistance/

Bröckling, Ulrich (2007): Das unternehmerische Selbst - Soziologie einer Subjektivierungsform, Suhrkamp.

Bröckling, Ulrich (2015): The Entrepreneurial Self: Fabricating a New Type of Subject, Sage 2015.

Brown, Wendy (1993): Wounded Attachments, in Political Theory, Vol. 21, No. 3 Aug., 1993, pp. 390-410.

Bührmann, Andrea D. (2005): The Emerging of the Enterprising Self and it's Contemporary Hegemonic Status: Some Fundamental Observations for an Analysis of the (Trans-)Formational Process of Modern Forms of Subjectivation, in Forum: Qualitative Social Research [On-line Journal], 2005, 6 (1).

Chen, Wei-Ping (2019): Review of 'Rated Agency: Investee Politics in a Speculative Age' by Michel Feher (Zone Books), Lateral 8.1 (2019). Available from: https://csalateral.org/reviews/rated-agency-investee-politics-feher-chen/

Davies, Will (2018): The best books on Moral Economy (interview by Caspar Henderson). Available from: https://fivebooks.com/best-books/moral-economy-will-davies/

Feher, Michel (2015): Brave New World Redux. Available from: https://maxdeesteban.com/brave-new-world-redux/

Feher, Michel (2016): Belonging and Neoliberalism (interview by James Graham). Available from: https://uploads-ssl.webflow.com/5a88c2b9ff16fd 000105979b/5aac25cd51e22e372c34e5a8_belonging_and_ neoliberalism.pdf

Feher, Michel (2018): Rated Agency: Investee Politics in a Speculative Age, Zone Books, 2018.

Feher, Michel (2019-1): Left Melancholy, Neoliberalism, and the Investee condition.
Available from: http://www.publicseminar.org/2019/05/left-melancholy-neoliberalism-and-the-investee-condition/

Feher, Michel (2019-2): The political ascendancy of creditworthiness, Public Books 2019.
Available from: https://www.publicbooks.org/the-political-ascendancy-of-creditworthiness/

Friedland, Roger (2017-1): The value of institutional logics, in: (forthcoming) Topics and Issues from European Research, in G. Kruecken, C. Mazza, R. Meyer, P. Walgenbach, eds., Cheltenham, UK: Edward Elgar Publishing, 2017.

Friedland, Roger (2017-2): Moving Institutional Logics Forward: Emotion and Meaningful Material Practice.
Available from: https://journals.sagepub.com/doi/abs/10.1177/0170840617709307

Friedland, Roger (2018): What Good Is Practice? Ontologies, Teleologies and the Problem of Institution, in: M@n@gement 2018, vol. 21(4): 1357-1404.
Available from: https://www.cairn-int.info/article_p.php?ID_ARTICLE=E_MANA_214_1357

Ganz, John (2019): Nightmares of the Credit Regime, Review of 'Rated Agency: Investee Politics in a Speculative Age' by Michel Feher, March 28, 2019.
Available from: https://thebaffler.com/latest/nightmares-credit-regime-ganz

Gratton, Peter (2015): Company of One: The Fate of Democracy in an Age of Neoliberalism.
Available from: https://lareviewofbooks.org/article/company-of-one-the-fate-of-democracy-in-an-age-of-neoliberalism/

Haidt, Jonathan (2001): The emotional dog and its rational tail: A social intuitionist approach to moral judgment. Psychological Review. 108, 814-834, 2001.
Available from: https://www.motherjones.com/files/emotional_dog_and_rational_tail.pdf

Kamber, Richard (1978): Review of On Being Free, Frithjof Bergmann, Notre Dame 1977 in: Philosophy and Literature - Johns Hopkins University Press, Volume 2, Number 2, Fall 1978.

Kloeckner, Christian and Stefanie Mueller (2018): Financial times: Competing temporalities in the age of finance capitalism.
Available from: http://financeandsociety.ed.ac.uk/article/view/2735/3825

Konings, Martijn (2015): The emotional logic of capitalism – What progressives have missed, Stanford University Press.

Kotsko, Adam (2018-1), Neoliberalism's Demons: On the Political Theology of Late Capital, Stanford University Press.

Kotsko, Adam (2018-2): Bedeviled by neoliberalism, in: Stanford University Press Blog 2018.
Available from: https://stanfordpress.typepad.com/blog/2018/08/bedeviled-by-neoliberalism.html

Krippner, Greta (2005): The financialization of the America economy, in Socioeconomic Review 2005- 3, p 173-208.
Available from: http://www.hr.fudan.edu.cn/_upload/article/b5/5e/e816d9f3439c946642016999bf90/b40e0f40-6867-43e0-83c5-5c1107dbe24e.pdf

Mennell, Stephen (2015): Sociogenesis and Psychogenesis: Norbert Elias's Historical Social Psychology as a Research Tradition in Comparative Sociology, 2015.
Available from: https://www.researchgate.net/publication/284398344_Sociogenesis_and_Psychogenesis_Norbert_Elias's_Historical_Social_Psychology_as_a_Research_Tradition_in_Comparative_Sociology

Overwijk, Jan (2018): Fantasies of Neoliberalism: From the Clerical to the Entrepreneurial Subject, in: Krisis, Issue 1, 2018.
Available from: https://krisis.eu/fantasies-of-neoliberalism-from-the-clerical-to-the-entrepreneurial-subject/

Petit, Phillip (2003), Agency freedom and option freedom.
Available from: https://www.princeton.edu/~ppettit/papers/Agency-Freedom_JournalofTheoretical%20Politics_2003.pdf

Pirsig, Robert M. (2006): Zen and the Art of Motorcycle Maintenance: An Inquiry into Values (1974), Harper Collins.

Stachowiak, J (2018), Review of The Entrepreneurial Self.
Available from:, https://www.academia.edu/32003479/_The_entrepreneurial_self._Fabricating_a_new_type_of_subject_Book_review

Stiglitz, Joseph (2019-1): Market Concentration Is Threatening the US Economy, Project Syndicate, March 11, 2019.
Available from: https://www.project-syndicate.org/commentary/united-states-economy-rising-market-power-by-joseph-e-stiglitz-2019-03

Stiglitz, Joseph (2019-2): Neoliberalism must be pronounced dead and
   buried. Where next? In The Guardian, 30 May 2019.
   Available from: https://www.theguardian.com/business/2019/may/
   30/neoliberalism-must-be-pronouced-dead-and-buried-where-
   next

Tongeren, Paul van (2001): Mens zijn in relaties: erkenning en zorg, in:
   Streven 68 (2001)11, p. 963-973.

Wikipedia: Michael Heinrich, in https://de.wikipedia.org/wiki/Michael_
   Heinrich_(Politikwissenschaftler)

Is Relational Thinking Wishful Thinking?[1]

By Johan Graafland

Introduction

THIS ESSAY WAS written as a commentary on the preparatory document for the conference 'The Power of Connectedness', which was organised by the Dutch Christian Social Congress. I will briefly summarise this preparatory document and emphasise its relevance from an economist's point of view. After this, I will make a number of critical comments on the idea of relational thinking. Finally, I will put forward an argument to look for the right balance.

'The Power of Connectedness'

The preparatory document for the congress is a well-written piece with a clear vision, calling us to action. It expresses concern that the current liberal way of thinking and – in its wake – the economic way of thinking assumes a caricature of human life. The most frightening part is that this caricature is actually brought to life by this very ideology. We depend too much on the idea that people are individuals who pursue their own interests in a rational way, as expressed in the view of the human being as a 'homo economicus'. Because there is insufficient attention to natural solidarity between people, and because institutions are organised according to this pessimistic view of human beings, we have started to act in accordance with this pattern. Institutions that focus on coercion and incentives drive out intrinsic motivations. In this way a tough society is formed, in which the other is seen as an enemy or opponent, and where ideology is transformed to bitter reality.

In order to set boundaries to this destructive force and to initiate a movement in the opposite direction, it is paramount to present relational alternatives. The document provides various examples in the form of case descriptions. Relationships are much more important to human happiness than economic growth. Human life can only flourish if people trust each other and collaborate. Human beings are social creatures and human dignity requires that people respect each other and care for each other. Institutions, both at the macro level and at the level of individual organisations, must be organised accordingly.

Connections to economic thinking

I find this vision very relevant and it is a good point of departure for this essay. An important insight already offered by Greek philosopher Xenophon, and later propagated by Adam Smith with his example of the pin factory, is that prosperity depends on the division of labour, both within the company and between companies and even countries. Xenophon therefore advocated treating foreigners with respect, not as enemies (Sedláček 2011). Labour productivity increases as a result of the division of labour, but we also become highly dependent on each other. We really, truly need each other. In order to make the division of labour possible, it is therefore crucial that an efficient exchange of goods and services is accomplished. Market imperfections such as inadequate information and external effects often exist. If so, the market can really only perform its task well if it is embedded in a social environment in which people can trust one another. Trust does not only make people happier (Graafland and Compen 2015), it also pays off in an economic sense. It is a prerequisite for achieving collective prosperity in a capitalist economy (Fukuyama 1995). Trust leads to openness and a willingness to close deals with other members of society. In addition, it reduces transaction costs. This is because high levels of trust require fewer checks and balances, as well as less detailed contracts or resources in the form of deposits or other guarantees to ensure the fulfilment of mutual obligations.

In the traditional economic view, social capital consists of a calculating type of trust. However, calculating types of trust may be insufficient to obtain the optimal social outcome from cooperative behaviour. Reputational considerations alone are not sufficient to yield the trust that is required to get relational contracts off the ground in dynamic, rapidly changing environments (Bovenberg 2003). If legal enforcement is lacking and the reputation mechanism is ineffective, the most favourable social outcome can only be obtained if both parties are truly committed to a voluntary agreement and refrain from cheating their trading partners even though they may reap pecuniary benefits from doing so. Trust is grounded in trustworthiness (Nooteboom 2017). If actors believe that their trading partners are trustworthy, they are willing to take risks and allow them freedom of action. For this reason, social preferences such as honesty, altruism, fairness, and commitment to common goals are important elements of the social capital, that foster economic development in a modern economy. Theoretical research also indicates that trust, combined with intrinsically motivated interest in the well-being of others - e.g. in the form of altruism or a preference for justice - leads to prosperity for all. This is because it makes it possible to overcome prisoner's dilemma-like conflicts of interest (Graafland 2007).

Institutions must therefore be structured in such a way that they promote so-called cooperative capitalism, in which cooperation and trust are central (Brand 2015). In the context of the Netherlands, you can think of the 'polder model' and sectoral consultations between employers' and employees' organisations. Such consultations facilitate agreements at a higher level that allow companies to compete at a lower aggregation level without neglecting collective interests. This is the so-called principle of ethical displacement. At the level of the individual company, too, institutions should be set up in such a way that the company is able to fulfil its social function well, with due regard for efficiency objectives that guarantee financial continuity.

Cooperative capitalism also makes it possible to facilitate social interaction outside the economic domain, for example by implementing agreements on collective rest. Social interactions contribute to people's social skills and stimulate intrinsic motivations and trust in one another (Graafland 2007). Another example of institutions that I believe promote social cohesion are institutions that make it possible for employees to work part-time. This allows parents to find a good balance between work as a means of self-development and the personal care for their children. The latter is an important condition for children to develop feelings of solidarity with others. A final example are institutions that make it possible to give people or companies new opportunities once they are trapped in a vicious circle of rising debts. Where people take responsibility for one another by sharing risks, the formation and consolidation of relationships is also stimulated. There are many other examples in which institutions lead to behaviour that reinforce relationships, and thus foster cooperative capitalism.

Connection to management theory

The importance of involvement is also reflected in management theories. Human management aims to promote involvement in the company. Involvement implies a sense of collective responsibility for the company that is not connected to the salary. People work not only for money, but also for a meaningful life. The natural need of people to be part of a larger social entity and to share things with others, as well as to create meaning in their own environment and to set goals that respond to those goals, are valuable to the company.

From this perspective, three levels of involvement can be distinguished. First of all, at the micro level, individual employees feel involved in their own task, with their own team, and with their own opportunities to develop their talents and make a career. The individual work context must be such that people can take their responsibility. At the meso level, employees feel involved in the internal organisation of business processes. They use their talents to positively influence these processes, think about how decisions are made, and how other employees can participate as well. Finally, at the macro organisational level, employees feel involved in the external functions of the company; for example, the relationship with customers, with other stakeholders, or with the public in general. Not every individual will be involved at all three levels. Nor is this necessary. It is important that everyone is involved to an extent that is both possible and useful. Meanwhile, people must not become too strongly motivated at the micro level. This would come at the expense of cooperation at the meso and/or macro levels. The art of leadership is to provide the context that makes such intrinsic involvement possible.

Companies that have a culture that promotes human management will also be more active in corporate social responsibility. This is evident from my own research based on a large survey of companies from twelve European countries. Companies that have a participatory management style are the ones most committed to corporate social responsibility (Graafland 2018).

Tension and balance between relational theories and reality

Is this the whole story? Does it not seem too good to be true? Does the notion of the importance of relationships in the economy not shatter on the hard surface of reality? Incidentally, this is also mentioned in the vision document. Examples abound. Volkswagen demonstrated great ideas for sustainability on its website, using terms like 'Think Blue', 'Blue Motion Technologies', and 'Volkswagen Responsible Driving'. Yet how did Volkswagen – until quite recently – earn most of its money? Not with technology that was 'Blue', but with technology that aimed at making consumers think they were 'Blue', meanwhile hiding how 'Black' they really were. We might wonder: what is the use of the business principles of big companies? Who would believe them?

It appears that the orientation on self-interest is more persistent in harsh economic reality than the vision document for the Christian Social Congress would have us believe. This raises two questions: whether relational thinking actually provides an adequate description of economic behaviour, and also – where this is not the case – if we should still set relational thinking as a standard. In grim reality, this could well be counterproductive. The reader may have heard of the 'Fable of the Bees' by Bernard de Mandeville (1806; first published 1714). He criticises the hypocrisy of his time in which vices were condemned, yet people wished to live in a rich society. According to De Mandeville, these two goals cannot exist alongside each other. If people live soberly, economic growth collapses and society implodes. Vice is necessary to stimulate the demand for and supply of goods and services.

I have been on the advisory board of a construction company for more than ten years. During this period, I have seen the consequences of the economic crisis for the construction industry from close by. Many companies went bankrupt. Not this particular company, however. This was not only because of the ethical standards of the company – in fact, it was more likely due to the hardworking people and managers in the company who considered their own wallet very important. Their financial motivation led to a very punctual way of working, in which cost levels were kept relatively low and good service was provided to customers. This resulted in good turnover and profit growth, notwithstanding the ongoing crisis. In all those years, not a single employee had to be fired.

The Gospel also suggests that one must be careful when exterminating evil. Greed is certainly an example of this. Tomáš Sedláček (2012) states in his book 'The economy of good and evil' that the Bible is aware of the fact that the suppression of evil can be counterproductive. He refers to the Parable of the Tares, in which Jesus says that weeds must not be removed because the good crop will also suffer. I believe this very issue exists in the economy; and it is an issue that any theologian, as well as any economist, must take into account.

We know that Adam Smith (2002; originally published 1759) strongly disagreed with De Mandeville and accused him of blurring the line between vice and virtue. Smith believed that man's own interests serve the social interest as if (s)he is led by an invisible hand, but he preferred to talk about these interests as a neutral concept or even as a virtue: the virtue of prudence. However, Smith comes perilously close to De Mandeville when he states that the corruption of human morality can have a positive effect on prosperity. For example, he points to the human tendency to have more sympathy for the rich and successful than for the poor. This is a corruption of morality within Smith's virtue-ethical framework, but according to him it is a corruption that we should cherish. Why? Because the positive focus on the rich encourages the less wealthy to also become rich. It activates them, and as a result, shared prosperity increases and everyone becomes happier. It seems as if we hear the echo of De Mandeville. This again demonstrates that relationships between ethics, wealth, and happiness are highly complex. It also shows that we must be careful when quoting Adam Smith as a support for our own views. This holds both for neoliberals - who picture Smith as the defender of a free market in which the self-interests of people can prevail - and for their opponents.

The question is how we can strike the balance in a reality where people often desire the good, yet act wickedly (see Romans 7). Of course, we must seize opportunities to strengthen trust relationships and intrinsic motivations as much as possible. However, where trust is abused, people must also be confronted with the consequences of their actions. Competition in the market and a good legal system that protects property rights are therefore important to safeguard justice and efficiency. The way the balance works out is also very much dependent on context. Societies and their cultures differ greatly. Depending on the nature of the market and on market imperfections, relational dimensions can be more or less suitable or necessary as a guideline.

1. This publication was made possible through the support of a grant from Templeton World Charity Foundation, Inc. The opinions expressed in this publication are those of the author and do not necessarily reflect the views of Templeton World Charity Foundation, Inc.

Bibliography

Bovenberg, A. L. 'Unity Produces Diversity. The Economics of Europe's Social Capital.' In *The Cultural Diversity of European Unity*, eds. W. Arts, L. Halman, and J. Hagenaars. Leiden: Brill, 2003.

Brand, T. *Coöperatief Kapitalisme*. Amsterdam: Buijten & Schipperheijn, 2015.

De Mandeville, Bernard. *The Fable of the Bees; Or, Private Vices, Public Benefits*. London and Edinburgh: T. Ostell and Mundell and Son, 1806.

Fukuyama, F. *Trust: The Social Virtues and the Creation of Prosperity*. New York: Free Press, 1995.

Graafland, J. J. *Economics, Ethics, and the Market. Introduction and Applications*. London: Routledge, 2007.

Graafland, J. J., and B. Compen. 'Economic Freedom and Life Satisfaction: Mediation by Income per Capital and Generalized Trust.' *Journal of Happiness Studies* 16.3 (2015): 789-810.

Graafland, J.J. 'Ecological Impacts of the ISO14001 Certification of Small and Medium-Sized Enterprises in Europe and the Mediating Role of Networks.' *Journal of Cleaner Production* 174 (2018): 273-282.

Nooteboom, B. *Vertrouwen. Opening naar een Veranderende Wereld.* Utrecht: Klement, 2017.

Sedláček, T. *Economics of Good and Evil. The Quest for Economic Meaning from Gilgamesh to Wall Street.* New York: Oxford University Press, 2011.

Smith, Adam. *The Theory of Moral Sentiments.* Cambridge: University Press, 2002.

Will Ethics Ever Trump Finance?

By Christiaan Vos

I MUST ADMIT that the title of this contribution poses a fairly odd question. It presupposes that there is an issue to be resolved with relation to finance, without explaining what the problem *within* finance might be. However, the question does suggest that ethics might be able to resolve everything. But why only finance, in that case? Should ethics not also trump corruption, or pollution, or resource depletion? Or does our question have a rhetorical component? Does it express a statement, a firm belief, that the role of ethics in society is to prevent all kinds of harm? I am convinced of the latter, and as such the answer to the question is a firm 'yes'. It could not possibly be otherwise. To understand how we could best place ethics at the center stage of the world of finance, we need to analyse the nature of the problem to be resolved.

Are things getting worse? Gordon Gekko, the unscrupulous Wall Street corporate raider brought to life by Michael Douglas in Oliver Stone's famous 1987 movie *Wall Street,* had the following motto: 'Greed is good!'. Unfortunately for him, and in spite of his personal beliefs, he is ultimately sentenced to jail for fraud. In the more recent sequel to Stone's film, *Wall Street: Money Never Sleeps* - staged around the 2008 financial crisis - the world seems to have changed. With a smug, villainous smile on his face, Gekko - now released from jail - notes that in today's society, greed even seems to be legal. He seems a little surprised.

The film is set in 2008, a year full of financial disasters. A major collapse of the financial industry was only barely prevented, mostly thanks to massive bank bailouts funded by taxpayers' money. 'Legalised greed' seems to have played a key-role in the events that led to the greatest financial crisis of our time. Was this failure of the free market the final proof that free market theories, in which greed plays a central role, are inherently flawed?

The Anglo-Dutch philosopher, political economist and satirist Bernard Mandeville argued in his famous *Fable of the Bees*, (1806; first published in 1714), that private vice will lead to public benefit. He claimed that virtue is actually detrimental to the state when it comes to commercial and intellectual progress. His philosophy caused great offence at the time, and was long stigmatised as false, cynical, and degrading – it was even considered to subvert morality (Mitchell 1911). However, some sixty years later Adam Smith took up a similar argument in *The Wealth of Nations*. He argued that 'it is not from the benevolence of the butcher, the brewer, or the baker that we expect our dinner, but from their regard to their own interest', which is led by an 'invisible hand' towards prosperity for all (Smith 1776). Free market theory was born.

Mandeville's fable and Smith's invisible hand have been of great influence on the design of the neoliberal world order in which we live today. They were supplemented by the ideas of influential figures like Austrian economist and political philosopher Friedrich von Hayek, who repeatedly praised the ideas of Mandeville (1981; see also Hayek 1967); the Russian-American novelist and philosopher Ayn Rand, who presented egoism as the highest virtue (1957; see also Rand 1961 and 1979); and Rand's greatest fan, former Chairman of the US Federal Reserve Alan Greenspan, who supported social security privatisation and immense tax cuts. The result: vice rules!

And why should it not? Mandeville explains clearly how virtuous behaviour will lead to the decay of a society. When his bees turned honest, the economy of the beehive collapsed. There was no need for locksmiths or policemen anymore and, due to the disappearance of envy and self-liking, the market for luxury goods came to a halt. However, greed did not prevent the crisis of 2008. We can agree that there was plenty of greed in the world at the time. Hence, vice should not rule.

We need to be careful when comparing the crisis in Mandeville's grumbling beehive with the 2008 financial crisis. And yet we could still draw conclusions doing exactly that. This is shown by Dutch economists Alexander Rinnooy Kan and Niels Achterberg. They point out that Mandeville did not claim that vice would *always* lead to public benefit. The same holds for Adam Smith. Both were aware of the need for capable politicians to introduce effective laws, ones that allow private vices to become public benefits, and at the same time prevent them from turning into public troubles (Kan and Achterberg 2009).

In a thought experiment, Rinnooy Kan and Achterberg speculate on how Mandeville would have reacted to the crisis of 2008. They argue that first of all, Mandeville would note that man has not changed over the past 300 years. The egoism postulated by Mandeville is still alive and kicking. Second, he would be enthusiastic about the vast body of knowledge economic science has produced on the topics of public welfare and the pursuit of individual interests. At the same time, he would be highly surprised that all this knowledge did not prevent lawmakers from entering into deregulation so easily. Third, therefore, Mandeville would advocate a stronger role for the government in the financial sector. In fact, this is the oft-forgotten essence of his theory, as well as that of Adam Smith: both stipulate that the state must play a central role.

The 2008 crisis was not caused by market failure

I do not think the 2008 crisis was caused by market failure. Markets functioned very well at the time. They were transparent, trade was prolific, profits were constantly increasing and bonuses were sky-high. The problem of under-priced credit risk was soon to be corrected by the market mechanism itself, had it not been for society to step in and save banks from bankruptcy. Why? Society had allowed markets to grow into massive financial conglomerates, and made itself dependent on them. This made banks too big to fail. Bankers and the financial markets were well aware of this.

Anat Admati, Professor of Finance and Economics at Stanford University, rightfully argues that 'many aspects of the financial system in developed economies are unjust because they allow powerful, better informed people to benefit at the expense of people who are less informed and powerful'. The system 'contributes to distortions in the distribution of income and wealth' and 'by allowing the privatisation of profits and the socialisation of losses, the financial system distorts basic notions of responsibility and liability' (Admati 2017).

Admati focuses on the so-called enablers of this 'dangerous financial system' who 'work within many organisations including auditors and rating agencies, lobbying and consulting firms, regulatory and government bodies, central banks, academia and the media'. The enablers, Admati argues, are part of the system and therefore have plenty reason to defend and propagate it. Their actions, or their failures to act, endanger and harm the public – even if some of them are actually charged with protecting the public. Some enablers are confused or misinformed, but according to Admati, this confusion is often wilful. Clientism and the protection of individual interest seem to prevent enablers from doing the right thing.

Dutch journalist Joris Luyendijk signalled something similar. His best-selling book *Swimming with Sharks* (2016) is an anthropological journey into the world of bankers. Luyendijk concludes that generally speaking, bankers are hardly ruthless, competitive, bonus-obsessed sharks. In most cases they are actually very nice and responsible people. Apparently, there is a mechanism at work in the sector of finance that transforms morally responsible people to amoral officials producing immoral outcomes.

Balance market, state and the people

The 'capable politicians' advocated by Mandeville and Smith, those who are supposed to set laws that guide private vice in producing public benefits while preventing public troubles, should not only focus on the financial industry as a system, but also on the individuals that work there. Our politicians should balance the market, the state, and people. Society must be protected. When laws allow for immoral outcomes, we should call upon the legislator to make better laws.

After the 2008 crisis we have seen that the pendulum of regulation swung towards more regulation. Internationally, the Basel III post-crisis reforms have set a new standard to strengthen the regulation, supervision, and risk management of banks. The quantity and quality of banks' regulatory capital was increased in order to make banks more loss-absorbent. Many jurisdictions reformed their legislation on prudential supervision of banks and introduced resolution frameworks that should prevent taxpayers from paying the bill for failing banks.

But will this be enough? We simply do not know. The new standard has yet to be tested by a systemic crisis. However, many argue that these new banking rules are not safe enough. Anat Admati and German economist Martin Hellwig (co-authors of *The Banker's New Clothes* (2013)), argue that the new risk-weighted capital requirements are still too soft. They suggest that a non-risk-weighted capital ratio of up to 30% is the only way to achieve a resilient and safe banking system.

Even if the current framework worked on a theoretical level, the danger lies in the fact that in practice, banking rules are very complex. This is one of the reasons that the pendulum of regulation is once again swinging back. The Trump administration, for example, recently weakened the Dodd-Frank banking rules. Perhaps even more importantly, the general complexity of rules is an open invitation to 'gaming' these very rules and exploiting loopholes through regulatory arbitrage.

Already in 1986, economist and laureate of the Nobel Memorial Prize in Economic Sciences Merton Miller said the following: 'The major impulses to successful innovations over the past 20 years have come, I am saddened to have to say, from regulation and taxes' (1986). He was recently quoted by Danièle Nouy, at that time chair of the Supervisory Board of the European Central Bank, when she delivered her speech 'Gaming the Rules or Ruling the Game? – How to Deal with Regulatory Arbitrage' (2017).

We should just do the right thing

Ethics might help answer the question posed by Nouy. Yes – we are in need of better laws. However, laws alone will not suffice. It is impossible to capture everything in law. The real world is so much more dynamic and complex than any law that might try to capture it. And laws usually lag behind. And even if we would find the ultimate law covering every single aspect of regulation, there would always be a boundary to that law. What are we supposed to do beyond this boundary? Might morality perhaps limit our options? Or do we live in a world where anything goes, unless it is forbidden?

There is an interesting scene in the 2012 movie *The Hunger Games*. Katniss Everdeen, the heroine of the story, is forced to participate in a life-or-death competition. A free-for-all is organised in which 24 players participate, but only one can win. The players are allowed – in fact, they are expected – to do whatever it takes to win the competition, including the killing of other players. They need to do so until they are the sole survivor and therefore victor of these 'hunger games'. In this particular scene, Katniss stumbles upon another player, whom she could kill quite easily. She decides not to. She does the right thing – she walks away. So does the other player. This is a moral action that takes substantial courage, because it is not without risk.

To make laws work properly – in the sense that they truly protect society –, people should not only apply the letter of the law, but also its spirit. Morality informs us about what is right and what is wrong – hence, morality can inform us on how to apply laws that are made to protect society. Really, we should just do the right thing.

However, this is easier said than done. In our ambitious and gains-driven society, morality is not risk-free. In a society where formal laws seem to trump moral laws, it will often be more profitable to cast aside moral concerns. This is what Admati warns of when she discusses enablers. And this is what Luyendijk observed happening in London city on a daily basis.

In our world of laws and lawyers, of formal rights and obligations, morality is pushed to the side-lines. But morality should always occupy the centre stage. It should be re-enabled to play its incredibly important role in the process of economic decision making and in people's economic lives. Companies are in need of morally sound decisions, but employees might not always feel protected enough to question the morality of certain business decisions.

Enable employees to bring morality to the workplace

Granted, when laws allow for immoral outcomes, we should call upon the legislator to come up with better laws. But we must think twice about the *kind* of laws we desire. Do we want more, and tougher, rules for banking? Maybe so. In addition to that, however, I propose another approach: to enable employees to bring morality to the workplace. This should be done not so much because it is the employees' duty to do so, but rather because it is their right. No employee should ever be forced to do things that are morally wrong.

Employees should be protected from moral corruption by the organisations they work for. Acknowledging the right of employees to question their employer's decisions based on moral standards could enrich labour law. Law could oblige employers to provide room for moral deliberation in the office. Seventeenth-century political philosopher Thomas Hobbes (1588–1679) contended that the sovereign had the 'whole power of prescribing the rules', to promulgate any civil law he might see fit to guard the 'publique peace' (1996: 125). I would hope my sovereign would see the need to enact laws that support and protect morality, enabling us all to do the right thing.

Bibliography

Admati, A. R. 'It Takes a Village to Maintain a Dangerous Financial System.' In *Just Financial Markets? Finance in a Just Society*. Ed. Liza Herzog. Oxford: University Press, 2017.

Admati, A. R., and M. Hellwig. *The Banker's New Clothes. What's Wrong with Banking and What to Do About It*. Princeton, NJ: University Press, 2013.

De Mandeville, Bernard. *The Fable of the Bees; Or, Private Vices, Public Benefits*. London and Edinburgh: T. Ostell and Mundell and Son, 1806.

Hayek, F. A. 'Dr. Bernard Mandeville: Lecture on a Master Mind.' Lecture, British Academy, 1960, London.

Hayek, F. A. *Law, Legislation, and Liberty*. Chicago, IL: University Press, 1981.

Hobbes, T. *Leviathan*. Rev. Student Edition. Ed. R. Tuck. Cambridge: University Press, 1996.

Luyendijk, J. *Swimming with Sharks. Inside the World of the Bankers*. London: Faber & Faber, 2016.

Miller, M. H. 'Financial Innovation. The Last Twenty Years and the Next.' *Journal of Financial and Quantitative Analysis* 21.4 (1986): 459-471.

Mitchell, J. M. 'Mandeville, Bernard de.' In *Encyclopædia Britannica,* 11th edition, ed. Hugh Chisholm. Cambridge: University Press, 1911.

Nouy, D. 'Gaming the Rules or Ruling the Game? How to Deal with Regulatory Arbitrage.' Speech, SUERF Colloquium, 15 Sep. 2017, Helsinki.

Rand, A. *Atlas Shrugged*. New York: Random House, 1957.

Rand, A. *Introduction to Objectivist Epistemology*. New York: First Mentor Printing, 1979.

Rand, A. *The Virtue of Selfishness*. New York: New American Library, 1961.

Rinnooy Kan, A., and N. Achterberg. 'Een Fabel over Hebzucht'. In *Boekenwijsheid. Drie Eeuwen Kunst en Cultuur in 30 Bijzondere Boeken*. Eds. Jan Bos en Erik Geleijns. Zutphen: Walburg Pers, 2009.

Smith, A. *An Inquiry into the Nature and Causes of the Wealth of Nations*. London: W. Strahan and T. Cadell, 1776.

PART 3

Relational Finance: Regulations, Policies, Practice

Reconnecting Finance and Society - About Rules and Purpose

By Theodor Kockelkoren

H OW DO WE reconnect finance with society? This is both an incredibly thorny and an incredibly important question. In this contribution, I will consider this question by drawing on my past experiences, in particular as a financial regulator at the Dutch Authority for Financial Markets (AFM), and my own perspectives.

My thesis is that society and finance will not reconnect if we continue to focus exclusively on rules and regulation, on supervisory structures, and on compliance. Of course these are important issues – however, they alone will not help us re-establish the connection between finance and society. Unfortunately, we must concede that the almost exclusive focus on rules and compliance persists widely, both in Europe and on a global scale.

This bias is consistent with the observation, made by among others a number of authors in the current publication, that we have been substituting relations for transactions for a few decades. We cherish rationality and calculation, we love the economic logic of self-interest, and we only barely accept law and regulation to keep us in check. Is it forbidden? No? Then go ahead and do your thing! This type of behaviour is perhaps the most fundamentally worrying aspect of the current rift between finance and society. Because *of course* finance is part of society. They are not two separate realms. The fact that finance and society are growing apart indicates the proliferation of different conceptions about values and purpose.

Including values and purpose in the equation

It is crucial that we discuss the issue of values and purpose. What do we stand for as a society? What do we find important? What is the economy meant for, and what should the financial sector stand for? How does finance contribute to society? These are very hard questions to pose in the public debate. In a society where divisions proliferate and anxiety is widespread, what chances remain for a real dialogue on values and shared purposes?

Are we willing to engage in such a dialogue? I fear that banks deem it very difficult to have this dialogue in any effective way in the present conditions. Nevertheless, the dialogue should take place, precisely because perspectives are so very different today. Society itself is of course heterogeneous, and so there will be segments that are closer to the financial sector than others when it comes to value and purpose. So it seems, at least – but we will only know if this is the case if we manage to engage in real dialogue.

Let me give a few examples. Society has clear and strong views on executive pay, which are not limited to the financial sector per se. Society also has expectations on the extent to which banks should be giving credit to households and to businesses. On the other hand, banks also have expectations, and they have their obligations. Banks have very clear views on the degree to which customers themselves are responsible for their actions, while society feels that banks should assume responsibility for the outcome. Can these differences be bridged? It is hard to say, but I feel that it is absolutely necessary that we try and engage in an honest dialogue. Our 'social contract' has already been damaged as a result of the crisis and might break completely if another significant crisis takes place. It is therefore safe to say that it is *absolutely urgent* that we come together on these issues.

Any dialogue starts with a willingness to listen, and to attempt to understand, one another. What is important to the other, what are the underlying and implicit assumptions of his/her reasoning? What are the values on which their arguments are based, and how do these contrast with my own values, my perspectives on the financial sector and my ideas on what finance should or should not be? There is no recipe on how to engage successfully in such a dialogue – we must simply try to open our minds and engage in honest conversation.

From rules and regulations to a dialogue on purpose

The question for purpose and values might begin and end with the role of the regulator. What should be the role of the regulator? I completely agree with Sylvester Eijffinger (see next chapter) that a regulator should do more than simply stick to the rules. Society has a purpose or ideal in mind when drafting a law and when formulating the regulations attached to this law. It is this purpose that needs to be realised in everyday societal practice. Adhering to the purpose of the law may not be as simple and straightforward as it seems. It demands reflection and creativity. Regulation and compliance can never be a simple matter of formulating and applying rules, of ticking boxes. I will not elaborate on this point here, chiefly because it would take a lot of space and also because I have already addressed the issue elsewhere (cf. Kockelkoren 2016). Please accept the premise that rule-based regulation will not win our common cause.

Instead, let me provide an example of how value-based regulation may work in practice. I am referring to the way the regulator (AFM) processed the report of the Dutch 'Maas' committee back in 2009. This committee was a so-called self-regulatory committee, brought to life by the Dutch Banking Association, that was tasked with providing recommendations for restoring societal trust in the banking sector. The committee's report caused a fundamental reorientation of banking practice. Among other things, customers' interests were once again made central to the banking process.

The pointed advice of the committee proved to be the kick-start for a dialogue between regulator AFM and banks and insurance companies. Questions that were asked were, for example: 'What does it mean to 'treat customers fairly', and what should be the implications of this in practice?'. The committee report triggered a dialogue we, at AFM, had always wanted to have. Finally, we were able to have a fruitful discussion with banks and insurance companies on how to translate the recommendations in the report not only to the board room, but also to the bottom level of customer representatives.

The first sessions were actually very difficult. Some interesting body language showed, on both sides. It took about three meetings before the different parties warmed to each other even slightly. The dialogue was very much helped by the fact that outside pressure was high. Everybody felt that something had to change. Outside pressure can really be a critical element in ensuring that difficult hurdles are taken. In this way, we were able to make significant progress and even continue to the practical level. At times, some of our dialogue partners would question whether the regulator was taking over the lead of their business. But then again – and take this from the institutions themselves – it was admitted that the dialogue was critical to have, and must continue.

To be clear, ours was not a dialogue on the rule of law. In fact, the law consists mostly of principles – it provided room for our dialogue. Only a handful of principles were involved and much of the dialogue focused on what these principles should mean in practice. It was never easy, but in the end we came to agree on the content of these principles and the applicable measures. Not just that: we were also able to agree on how both parties – financial institutions and the regulator – could track actual performance and the progress made in practice. We even agreed that the outcome of these monitoring reports would serve as input to continue the dialogue.

Of course, it would be easiest – and safest! – for the regulator to invoke very detailed regulation and stick to it, rather than leaving the rules aside and engage in a dialogue with the regulated parties. Looking across Europe, the approach of AFM was not a common one. But these are important issues for financial institutions, governments and societies – and a dialogue goes a long way in establishing good practice.

I am quite impressed by the European Central Bank (ECB) as an institution and by its efforts to improve the mechanisms of the European financial markets. However, their whole operation is generating a spiralling dynamics of ever increasing detail. Why? Because they have made consistency throughout Europe their highest goal, and they consider the invocation of detailed regulation the only way to guarantee this. I am not sure whether this is a good solution. Do we really want a 900-page supervisory protocol, as is currently the case?

Can we all act as human beings?

We require regulators that keep ideals in mind and are open to dialogues on purpose and value, and on how to convert them to everyday practice. In short: we require regulators with practical wisdom. This explains the concept of the so-called idealistic regulator. Such idealistic regulation can take the shape of a dialogue, provided businesses are ready to acknowledge that they are fundamentally embedded in society. I would like to refer once again to the notion of the social contract, as it contains a number of implicit elements by which we acknowledge that everyone is connected; that society is the sum of us all; and even that we are together on this planet. As a result, we have a shared responsibility.

If both regulator and businesses share this type of thinking, then it is possible to have a fruitful dialogue, a common engagement that goes far beyond economic terms and rational structures. All those issues are recast to include a human and societal perspective. This is where ethics comes in, and where rules and regulations take the backseat. I really do hope that we will be able to create more space for such encounters.

When meeting colleagues from all over Europe, I was often struck by their near-obsessive attention to rules, structures, compliance, and risk management approaches. However, many of these colleagues feel, both on a professional and on a personal level, that human, societal and ethical perspectives are indispensable. They lament the lack of space for these perspectives in the current framework. My call is therefore to create more space for professionals to act as human beings – whether they are regulators or working in the financial sector.

Bibliography

Kockelkoren, Theodor. *Toezicht als Beroep*. Gentian Publishing, 2016.

Restoring Trust

By Sylvester Eijffinger

IN DECEMBER 2016, the Dutch Monitoring Committee Banking Code presented its final report, titled 'Bridging the Gap'. The report states that trust in banks remains quite low; it ranks 2.6 on a scale from 1 to 5. The report also states that it is not clear which fundamental changes have taken place at the heart of the banking industry – in particular when it comes to the assessment of their own business activities. The monitoring committee therefore advises banks to instruct employees across the board on how to deal with ethical dilemmas. This could be done by conducting debates that span the different layers of the organisation.

When reading the report, I could not help but reflect on the activities of the 'Maas' committee back in 2009, of which I was a member. The task of our committee was to *contribute to responsible and sustainable banking*, and its final report, titled Restoring Trust, largely dealt with the same subject matter as this new report.

I would like to offer my reflections on the present-day discussions in light of our 2009 report; i.e. how our report came about, what its insights and conclusions were, and to what extent I believe it is still relevant in the present day, even if nine years have passed.

Bad risk management and poor governance

In autumn 2008, the Dutch Cabinet was working hard to rescue several banks that were on the brink of bankruptcy. Meanwhile, there was an urgent need for a committee to provide advice on policies that could redress the problems in the financial sector. Then Minister of Finance, Wouter Bos, together with the chairman of the Association of Dutch Banks, Boele Staal, installed the 'Maas' Committee. This committee was composed of three seasoned bankers and one professor, the latter being myself. There was a strict timeline to our report: it had to be delivered within the space of three to four months. The first month was spent discussing the nature of the report we sought to deliver. This was not self-evident, because the other three members of the committee held high positions in their respective financial institutions, and as such had to take into account the interests of their stakeholders. Together, we had to construct a 'house' of sorts – but first, we had to find a shared foundation.

At last, we found something that might work. Our foundation would be a book called 'De Prooi' (The Prey), by Jeroen Smit (2009). It is a beautiful book that describes the decline and almost-fall of ABN AMRO, and was a bestseller at the time. Its conclusion is simple and straightforward: the lethal combination of bad risk management and poor governance was the underlying cause of the decline of ABN AMRO, and indeed of many other banks. Bad risk management and poor governance: these were to become the focus of our Committee's research and report. Governance here refers to what the Dutch call 'intern toezicht': the disciplinary role of the executive and – especially – the supervisory board.

The work of the 'Maas' Committee should be understood against this background. We were given the task of contributing to practices of responsible and sustainable banking, and so we focused on the entwined problems of bad risk management and poor governance. I stress this point because I think these two problems remain largely unresolved today. I also stress it because both the press and the public debate that followed publication of our report focused on other topics in the report entirely: their main attention was devoted to issues that we considered of minor importance, such as the bankers' oath and the need to once again make the customer's interest the primary goal of banking practice. These recommendations were not the principle message of our report. And it is a pity that they were understood to be so important, because the core message was subsequently lost sight of – even though it is as relevant today as it was back in 2009.

Banks are strange and complicated creatures

So what did we do? We started by reflecting on the peculiar nature of banks. Banks are very strange animals. They are in charge of the payment system, and as such they have a public utility function. This public utility function was the main reason they needed to be saved when the crisis hit. But in order to be sustainable, a bank must also be efficient. The old 'spaarbanken' (credit unions) disappeared because they were not efficient enough. The result of these two aspects of the bank is a peculiar combination of public utility and commercial efficiency, causing the bank to service different stakeholders at the same time.

But there's more to this strange animal. The heart of the banking business today consists of managing the very delicate balance between profitable commercial activities and risk management. It is a character-istic activity for banks. Internally, executives and the supervisory board are in charge; externally, the Dutch Central Bank (DNB) and the regulator, the Authority for Financial Markets (AFM). This is where things went wrong: neither the internal nor the external control mechanisms for risk management functioned properly. Why not?

The risk appetite of a bank is one of its defining features. To decide on risk appetite is above all a strategic act: it decides what kind of bank you are. The risk appetite of a retail or consumer bank is completely different from the risk appetite of a private or an investment bank. If a bank chooses to have a very high risk appetite, it runs the risk of not qualifying for the deposit insurance system offered by the DNB.

The heart of the matter: defining the risk appetite

There are two aspects to deciding the risk appetite of a bank. Risk decisions are taken on a daily basis by the executive board, but their policies must be approved by the supervisory board. The latter serves as the internal control and disciplinary mechanism of the bank – a checks and balances system of sorts is in place. In short, the supervisory board, in communi-cation with the executive board, defines the risk appetite of the bank.

I would like to stress that even today, there is no full recognition of the fact that a bank is the most complicated animal of all business creatures in existence. A bank has to manage all kinds of risk: credit risk, liquidity risk, operational risk, et cetera. These risks operate on two sides: assets and liabilities. One need only consider the documentation provided at supervisory board meetings to see how complicated the bank's business is. Normal companies have a regular pile of documents, but for banks this pile could easily be ten times as big. The sheer complexity of the banking business calls for solid and sophisticated governance and the proper functioning of the two-layered system: that of the executive board and the supervisory board working in tandem.

In order for this system to function properly, an executive board with solid expertise is required; as well as a supervisory board that is fully aware of its critical function in the process, and is up to the task; and finally, open and fluent communication between the two layers that orchestrate the smooth running of these core mechanisms of the bank.

In all three of these aspects there were – and I believe, still are – serious flaws. Probably the weakest link, however, is the supervisory board. I think it does not properly fulfil its crucial function. Why not? The main reason is that a good supervisory board member should possess a wide range of critical skills. You must have expertise; you must be independent; you have a solid character; and finally, you must dedicate sufficient time to the job. There seems to be insufficient awareness that to be a supervisory board member for a bank is an incredibly serious and highly complicated job.

The regulator – stuck in regulation

Now let us have a look at risk management and the role of external supervisors, that is the Dutch Central Bank and the Authority for Financial Markets. For a number of years directly after the onset of the crisis, banks were much more cautious when taking risks. Some promising steps were taken in the right direction, including defining and circumscribing risk appetite and balancing the risks. However, developments in the past few years clearly indicate a return to the pre-crisis situation.

This negative turn is triggered, I would say, by the way external regulation is exercised. Regulation in the Netherlands is of a rule-based type, which hampers – or at the very least fails to incite – any serious research and reflection beyond the rules. Instead, we have ended up with box-ticking exercises. For external supervision to really function, regulation should be principle-based. Why? Because principle-based regulation requires the regulator to know what is *really* happening at the bank. Supervisory authorities like the AFM and the DNB would then be obliged to recruit and train people who understand the banking business, who have worked for a bank in the past, and who are aware of possible dilemmas and of possible tricks of the trade.

Conclusion

As I have stressed repeatedly in this contribution, risk management is a very complicated affair, meaning that the supervision of risk management – internally, by the supervisory board, or by the external supervisors – can only be very complicated as well. This task can only be performed by seasoned, experienced professionals with a solid character. There is no escaping that. But instead, we encounter all kinds of talk about psychology; about group and boardroom dynamics; and more. All of these are certainly relevant – and when it comes to recruiting new board members for the bank or the regulator, this knowledge results in all kinds of qualifications listed on the job description. What we really need, however, are experienced professionals with a solid character.

Bibliography

Smit, Jeroen. *De Prooi. Blinde Trots Breekt ABN AMRO.* Amsterdam: Prometheus, 2009.

Pension Funds for the Common Good

By Carla Moonen

FROM 2013 TO 2016, I was chair of the Water Authority 'Brabantse Delta', in the south of the Netherlands. The 21 water authorities in the Netherlands are autonomous bodies, though they are publicly controlled, for example through the democratic election of their boards. The Netherlands has a long history of working both against and with water, and the Dutch water authorities are amongst the oldest national public institutions - some of them dating back to the middle of the thirteenth century. Because of their particular histories, as well as their important tasks, the authorities have the right to collect public taxes on their own.

In my work for the water authority, I experienced how important it is for a chairperson to know first-hand what the people you are working for really need and want. In the area of the 'Brabantse Delta' water authority there was a significant number of people living directly behind the dikes. Many of them lived in areas that had been heavily damaged by floods in past centuries, particularly the so-called 'Big Flood' of 1953 (a national disaster, killing 1836 people in the south-western provinces of the Netherlands). In my conversations with the people living in these areas, many of them urged me to invest their tax money in long-term investments for water security. So we did. In the beginning of 2018, these and other Dutch long-term investments in water security proved extremely useful. The levels of the Rhine and Maas rose to exceptional heights, yet everyone in the region kept their feet dry.

In 2016, I changed jobs, and I became chair of the second-largest Dutch pension fund, PFZW. This pension fund is responsible for the pensions of 2.7 million employees in the Dutch Healthcare and Welfare Sector, and it invests nearly €200 billion worldwide. The Dutch population stands at 17 million, and as such virtually everyone in the country knows someone who works in this sector. Generally speaking, this 'someone' is a person who works hard but gets paid little: average earnings in the sector are below the average national wage. And yet they dedicate their life to the care for others. In my new function it became my job to manage these peoples' pension savings, and therefore to take care of their financial future.

As part of my introduction to the field, I had conversations with a lot of people that work in the sector. In one of my first weeks on the job I visited the north-eastern province of Drenthe and made the acquaintance of a geriatric nurse. I asked her what was important to her when it comes to her pension savings. Her answer confirmed the findings of much of our research among our members: her main interest with regard to old age provision was to have a degree of security. She would even accept a slightly lower monthly pension pay-out if that meant she could be reasonably sure about the height of the provision. She then pointed to one of her younger colleagues and asked me to make sure that her own pension would not be paid at the expense of the pension of that colleague. It struck me that this nurse, like the vast majority of our members, was not in favour of enormous differences between 'lucky' and 'unlucky' generations, but preferred solidarity instead.

My conversations with members all over the country showed me that members of the PFZW pension fund prefer long-term security over short-term profits. They want their pension to be secure. They prefer solidarity over individuality and wish to make sure that each generation gets a fair share. Moreover, it became clear to me that they want to live in a beautiful rather than a polluted and destroyed world – now and after retirement. This may sound like common sense, yet we seem not to think about the consequences of these wishes. Luckily, this is changing gradually.

PFZW is embedded in the financial sector, and as such a central questions we asked ourselves is the following: 'How do we translate the wishes of our members, and therefore of society, to the functioning of the financial markets?' and 'How can we deliver stable pensions for all generations and avoid being easily affected by imbalances in the financial sphere (as is currently the case)?'

How can pension funds become more resilient to imbalances in the financial sphere?

In my job as chair of the Water Authority, as well as at PFZW, I experienced that the answer to basic questions is to be found among the people that one serves. In both cases, people asked for long-term investments in a better world. They asked for solidarity. And they asked us to invest in companies that improve the world. If pension funds follow these guidelines, they will be able to provide their participants with a good pension and make the world a better place.

In essence, the investment policy of any pension fund is this: to profitably cover all years until pensions will have to be paid out. For most funds, this period spans decades. This means that these investments are inherently long term. However, at PFZW, the investment strategy is also characterized by its focus on sustainability: the desire to contribute to a better world. This has not been without results. PFZW has been voted the most sustainable pension fund in the Netherlands eleven times in the last twelve years. To illustrate this: at PFZW, I have been involved in the process of investing €14 billion, about 7% of all invested assets, in companies and projects which provide solutions for pressing problems in society. The goal is to raise this amount to €20 billion (about 10% of all invested assets), in 2020. Our investment policy was based on the United Nations' Sustainable Development Goals (SDGs), especially those related to *climate, water, health* and *food*. To this end, we selected companies that had a measurable positive impact on one of these issues. At PFZW, it is believed that a long-term focus on sustainability (on the part of both investors and companies) has the associated effect of generating better financial results. This in turn is necessary for the pension fund to pay out adequate pensions. This fits in very well with the convictions of our members, who believe that money alone does not buy a decent retirement. Furthermore, by focusing on companies that aim at long-term value creation we could exercise a stabilizing role on financial markets.

How can society become more resilient to imbalances in the financial sphere?

Society has become very dependent on the financial sector. As a result, it has become very sensitive to imbalances in the financial world. Reducing this dependency will make society more resilient to financial crises and the procyclical impulses originating from the financial sector. To achieve this, countervailing power on the demand side – the citizenry - needs to be strengthened further.

Do the members of PFZW want to be solely dependent on the results of the stock market for their pension? I think it would be fair to say that PFZW members have a clear view on this matter. 85% of the members are female and 60% of them earn less than the average worker. These members support the fund's sustainable investment policy and they do not wish to see their money invested in complex financial products that do not serve the real world. They prefer to share in a fair and equitable way in the financial results of the fund's investment policy, and wish to see an equal pension for equal work. By focusing on the long term, and therefore by following the wishes of their members, pension funds can play an important stabilizing role in financial markets.

What are the perspectives for a proper arrangement between the financial sector, state, and society?

Building on the preferences of the fund's own members I see three possibilities for such partnerships.

First of all, institutional investors like PFZW can contribute to financial stability by investing only in financial instruments that are easy to understand, easily managed, and serve real, sustainable goals. At PFZW we therefore stopped investing in hedge funds and complex financial derivatives. Second, we need a new pension system in the Netherlands: one that enables pension funds to fully exploit their potential for long-term investment. This means that the current arrangements and supervisory rules, which are procyclical in nature, need to be replaced by a new system that enables pension funds to perform a stabilizing role.

Third, a true partnership between financial sector, state and society would enable investments to be in line with the goals of society as a whole, such as the required transition to green energy. To achieve this, the state needs to develop a long-term vision and create the right framework conditions for pension funds and other long-term investors, such as pension funds, to step up. This calls for a form of public-private partnerships.

It is my belief that the idea of a proper European financial-societal arrangement should receive new attention. Based on my own experience, this can be stimulated by returning to the wishes of our members – to society – and then using the autonomy of pension funds to bring investment policies in line with these wishes. I believe this is a search for a measure of freedom for institutions to manoeuvre in a complex financial environment, guided by the wishes of their own members.

In my professional experience in government positions (at the Water Authority) as well as in the financial sector (at PFZW), I have learned that societal interests should always be taken into account. When dealing with rather complex issues - like water- or pension management – it often helps to start by simply gathering the wishes of constituents or participants.

A Broad Approach to Finance and the Common Good

By Steven Vanackere

RATIONALITY IS THE new honourability. Thus far, we have insisted on discovering the causes of – or better, the *reasons for* – the recent global financial crisis. However, by looking for reasons, we invite modernity to the stage, along with its compelling focus on goal-instrumental action. I am convinced that a less economised rationality will provide us with more than just a hint of authentically new directions for the financial sector. We would discover a rationality with more focus on values, emotions, and even tradition.

There is a very peculiar assumption at the core of so-called rational choice theory. This theory presumes that the behaviour of rational agents simply consists of always seeking maximisation in the pursuit of their own material wealth. It presumes that any act that is not opportunistically motivated should be judged irrational.

That view is problematic when it comes to human motivation – Bruno Frey aptly demonstrates this in his work *Not Just for the Money* (1997). I would like to expand on Frey's observations by arguing that civilisation enters a new phase when pause is pressed on the *do ut des* reciprocity: I give – or I refrain from taking advantage of you – not because you are able and willing to reciprocate, but because you, as a human being, are worth it.

It is too easy for us to simply declare the financial sector guilty, and to forget that – if there were a trial to be had – all of the economy is implicated. Let me provide three examples:

1) The capitalistic free market still fails to create a just market price, one that fully integrates the societal cost of externalities;
2) Worldwide, there is huge asymmetry in sharing the economic value chain;
3) The abuse of economic power through monopolies; the injustice and violence that come with the current resource rush on this planet (which includes food speculation).

All of these plagues are problems of the real economy, and not just of the world of finance. What we require is a fundamental change in perspective – we need to put people at the centre of our sense of purpose.

The financial sector has an irreplaceable role to play in developing sound economies. It is a noble vocation to redistribute money and risks in the economy, so as to make sure that good ideas get proper funding and that human progress can take its course. Once the banker loses sight of this sense of purpose, and starts thinking that he or she is only in business to make profit and please stock markets, there is something profoundly wrong.

In the years leading up to the banking crisis, there was a quite generalised myopia preventing people from seeing much further than the performance charts in the stock exchange. The aggravating circumstance was blatant short-termism, inspired by a very short-sighted incentive model, both for employees, executives and companies in general.

What about today? Sometimes I feel that only the rush to perform on the short term has – at least to some degree – been problematised and dealt with, but that the rest of the model remains the same. Instrumentalisation is still rampant. Shareholders' value is still central, even though it is far from synonymous to 'value' in general.

Values such as integrity cannot (and should not) be bought. I am aware that many people believe ethical behaviour is in a company's best interest – notably because of the reputational damages caused by unethical behaviour – and that some would like to install ethics as an instrument of competition. This idea has given rise to what we might call, perhaps slightly disparagingly, an 'ethics industry', with consultants and coaches, courses and seminars. All of these try to prove that a company that takes ethics seriously stands a better chance of turning a good profit.

There are two things fundamentally wrong with this. First, ethics cannot be outsourced by the leadership of a company - not to the best consultant in the world, not to your excellent subordinates and most certainly not to a PR company. Integrity cannot be bought. One cannot shift moral responsibility, because it is directly related to leadership. Neither can one shift moral responsibility; it has to live in each and every position within the company. The second problem with the idea of ethics as a tool for prospering businesses is that ethics should not be instrumentalised – even when one stretches the time scale to its utmost, and is extremely patient in harvesting the sweet fruits of integrity. Why? Because simply put, there will be times where doing the right thing costs money – and continues to cost money in the long run.

Of course, regulation is all-important in providing for minimal standards. These can install an indispensable knowledge in the sector that noncompliance to these standards will never grant a competitive advantage. All the same, I would like to point out several fundamental drawbacks that exist in the practice of regulation. First, there is the annoying red tape - the administrative complications - that undoubtedly ensue when regulation comes into play. The transaction costs of compliance and enforcement are important and widely underestimated.

Second, there is a real danger of what I call the 'ethical substitution' effect. Let me provide an example from a field study carried out by the Israel Institute of Technology in 1998, presented in 2000 in their paper 'A Fine is a Price'. In a group of day-care centres, a monetary fine was introduced for parents who were late, as parents picking up their children after closing time were forcing personnel to stay late. After the fine was introduced, the number of parents arriving late... increased significantly! The theory that explains this is that parents believe the social contract is superseded by the establishment of a scheme of fines: they now know the 'price' of their behaviour. They feel the fine compensates for the hassle provoked by their actions. They now believe it is up to the management of the day-care centre to compensate their employees for having to work late, rather than feeling responsible on a personal level.

A third drawback is the problem of regulatory competition between nation states. Forces of globalisation and of economic and financial liberalisation have put tremendous pressure on the Rhineland model – the socially and ecologically corrected market economy. This is because the model relies heavily on governments that are willing and able to impose such corrections. The tragedy (a so-called 'tragedy of the commons') is that not a single country is willing to make these sacrifices, or to impose limits on its own behaviour, merely for the sake of the global common good. Economic game theory explains how countries get caught up in a prisoner's dilemma, based on a seemingly rational expectation process concerning the behaviour of the other 'partners in the game'. Solving free-rider problems will continue to rely on international agreements, in which signatory states effectively impose limits on themselves and the other signatories. I believe that continued progress in terms of account-ability and stronger enforcement of freely accepted commitments is the most realistic way forward. Our planet needs a kind of 'transactional sovereignty', or 'contractualisation of sovereignties' if you will.

My final thoughts concern the European integration process. After World War II, the initial engine of the peace process – the integration of economies and financial markets - seems to have completely taken over from the more value-inspired project of an increasingly united Europe. The engine *became* the project. For some, the European Union is a market, rather than *having* a market.

I am convinced that our European future will be constructed in an even more hybrid, asymmetrical and less linear way than we have considered up to this point. Notwithstanding the understandable allergies to a 'Europe à la carte', I think it is unavoidable that different nations will find themselves at different levels of integration. One can only hope that in the heart of this Europe, there will be enough room for *Wertrationalität* ('value rationality'). This has to do with the ways in which we educate our children, involve our civil society, respect the human sense of religion, cherish our intellectual, artistic, literary and philosophical community and define sound politics. All of these things have to do with a sense of morality, character and the capacity to be critical of oneself. If we really wish to live together, we best make these decisions together.

Bibliography

Frey, Bruno. *Not Just for the Money. An Economic Theory of Personal Motivation.* Cheltenham: Edward Elgar, 1997.

Gneezy, Uri, and Aldo Rustichini. 'A Fine Is a Price.' *The Journal of Legal Studies* 29.1 (2000): 1-17.

PART 4

*Relational Finance in
the World of Tomorrow*

Ethics of FinTech: The Need for a Normative Debate Before the Computer Says 'No'

By Maarten Biermans

Introduction

ANYONE VISITING LONDON might very well find themselves walking down Waterloo Road, crossing the Thames at Waterloo Bridge or perhaps taking a train at Waterloo Station. All of these landmarks were named in honour of the victory of the Duke of Wellington over Napoleon Bonaparte at the battle of Waterloo in 1815. Comparable testaments to this battle are found across Europe, e.g. in Amsterdam, Osnabrück, and Brussel. With so many monuments, it is somewhat ironic that referring to someone's Waterloo nowadays means to refer to someone's (ultimate) defeat.[1] It almost seems that the defeat of Napoleon at Waterloo is considered more impressive than the victory achieved by his opponents, Wellington and Von Blücher – monuments commemorating the latter notwithstanding.

This notion – that of the changing meanings of concepts in everyday language – can arguably also be applied to the concept of humanity. For example, the authors of an introductory chapter to a course book on business ethics noted that the reader need not worry about whether they would do a perfect job all the time, saying: 'You will make mistakes, after all, you are only human'. Here, humanity is expressed in a similar way to various everyday expressions, such as: 'I am only human', or 'Nothing that is human is alien to me'. It would seem that a subtle alteration of Rene Descartes' insight is at play here: we move from his 'I think, therefore I am' to 'I am, therefore I make mistakes'. The human measure is made to be a measure of imperfection. This latter observation is a perfect point of entry for any discussion on FinTech - or artificial intelligence in general - given that tackling these human imperfections is part and parcel of its *raison d'être*.

FinTech: the 'how' does matter

There is a vast array of works on the potential opportunities of FinTech, one that grows every day. However, contributions - and indeed the debate itself - on the normative dimension of FinTech are still very limited. Of course, one might readily counter: 'Why should there be such a debate in the first place? If FinTech is merely a tool to advance wellbeing, why would we have a normative discussion about it? We do not have any normative discussions about gardening tools, so why should be there be one about this new technological toolset that will help us in our financial dealings? The general promise of FinTech is that it will help us deal with our financial chores faster, smarter and cheaper; what could possibly be wrong with this?'

The answers to these questions lie – as they do in many other cases – in the sphere of the ancient debate on means and ends. In this case it is not so much about the 'what' (although that too remains important) but more about the 'how', i.e. 'How' does FinTech help us achieve greater well-being? Even if we agree on the goal, there is still the question of the desirability of the resources deployed and the way in which these resources are used in order to achieve this goal. In that sense, this debate closely mimics the debate on the nature of the quest for justice, namely: does the manner in which justice is realised matter? Should the way to achieve justice not be as much subject to our moral deliberation as the question of the foundation of justice itself? If the assumption is that it does, then this constitutes a clear point of entry for the need of a normative debate on FinTech. The next section explores some of the context of this debate, as well as some of the themes that might be explored.

The financial crisis

For any contemporary discussion on ethics and finance it is nigh on impossible to bypass the recent financial crisis and its fall-out. In 2008, financial institutions such as banks brought the financial system to the edge of the abyss. Even before the dust had settled, one bank after another promised to mend their ways and improve the manner in which risk and governance were embedded in the overall system. Banks also pledged to recalibrate their moral compass. In some countries, such as Australia and the Netherlands, a separate banker's oath was introduced in which the social importance of the banker's role is explicitly mentioned. In short, the normative discourse that was successfully kept outside the gates of financial institutions for so long was now (under public pressure) becoming part of the overall management of these same institutions.[2]

A notable part of this process of reflection and atonement by the financial sector, and of the banks in particular, was the recognition that the interests of the client should become more central in the overall operations. Banks (again) realised and acknowledged that they have a responsibility towards the customer.

As is often the case with important changes, this major shift in thinking was accompanied by what may ultimately turn out to be a much bigger development, namely the advance of FinTech. Interestingly, the emergence and early successes of FinTech actually showed to some extent that the client or customer is not necessarily anxiously awaiting the newly found sense of responsibility of the banks towards them. Why? Because the new bank (apparently) does not have a network of offices across the country, but fits in the back pocket of a pair of jeans: it is the smartphone. In this way, the advance of FinTech is accompanied by a sense among customers that banks and financial institutions are to deliver on specific tasks, and apart from this, should keep to themselves, move out of the way and not be a hindrance. By introducing more efficiency in the overall service to clients, FinTech in some way has reduced the role of the financial service provider to precisely that: the provider of services. Again, this begs the question: how is there a normative challenge to any of this? One example of where this questions presents itself is when it comes to the duty of care of a bank towards its clients. The basic idea is that banks have a duty to ensure that their clients are well looked after. This duty – which in the Netherlands has even become part of the job description of the regulatory bodies – can be seen as an expression of the idea of the social function of a bank, in which the bank takes the interests of its clients and third parties into account. Is this 'duty of care' something that we can apply to new players in the FinTech scene? And if so, who holds this duty? And who will determine the meaning of *care* in this space? Ideally, these questions are debated well before the manifestation and further embedment of FinTech in the financial sector presents itself as a *fait accompli*.

Future views

FinTech is already proving itself to be a very effective support to the standard service offering of banks and to overall financial services, for instance through the integration of more (relevant) information in customer profiles. Surely nobody would complain about this? After all, FinTech improves the delivery of services and possibly even strengthens the already mentioned duty of care. To illustrate the latter, imagine the following case. What should be done with a customer who wishes to take out a loan with the bank, even though the latter can now see (based on all sorts of linked databases) that this customer's most recent cash withdrawals were all in, or next to, a casino in the middle of the night? From a pure risk perspective, it may not be a very good idea for the bank to facilitate the loan. Surely this sounds like very prudent behaviour on the part of the bank? But what if the nature of 'big data' becomes even more predictive, i.e. by way of incorporating big data analysis, neuro-linguistics computing, and more? What if the causality of actions can no longer be recognised with the proverbial naked eye? Then what? Do we not run the risk of slowly moving towards a situation wherein the notion of statistical discrimination has been elevated to a business plan, though in a manner so deeply buried in algorithms that only another algorithm could uncover it? What if this is indeed the case – what if this is what the future holds? What type of supervision and regulation is going to be put in place to remedy this – another algorithm?

These last questions may sound alarmist. In some sense, however, the writing is very much already on the wall. With the rise of Artificial Intelligence, the risk of Artificial Stupidity also increases, e.g. seeing connections and relationships that are in fact not (yet) real. We need to speak in normative terms about the undesirability of certain types of analysis *before* they manifest themselves as firmly integrated in the financial sectors. Should we wait until our FinTech App rejects a loan application based on your Spotify playlists of the past week, say, because it was just a bit too suicidal or slightly too licentious?

In Dutch, there is an expression (the literal translation of which reads 'I do not steal from my own wallet') that people invoke to indicate that they are not likely to miss out on a good (financial) opportunity. But what if we find ourselves in a situation where this expression actually decides your overall credit score? What if an algorithm would be able to determine that you actually regularly miss out on good business opportunities? And what if this clear lack of action in accordance with rational self-interest is then included in the algorithm that decides on a loan for your new business? The result will be that the 'computer says no'.

In the past, various economists have lamented the fact that real people rarely act in accordance with economic models based on rational self-interest. If an algorithm actually includes this criterion in its own deliberations and output, being a thief of your own wallet might actually become an outlawed activity. In other words, we must ask: will the algorithm allow us to make judgements based on morality, or will it punish us if anything but profit maximisation is acted on?

I must emphasise here that the algorithms I refer to are not necessarily the ones we humans can (and already do) create. I am referring to algorithms that have been created by other algorithms – without human interaction – and that are updated a billion times every second. This in turn raises the question of whether it is possible to code for morality.

Can we code for morality?

As mentioned earlier, the idea that 'being human' has various negative connotations in everyday language – mainly as an expression of imperfection – is familiar. There are, of course, exceptions to this. One of the most striking of these is the way in which humanity is used to justify deviation from well-defined rules. For example, one can easily imagine a comment on a court sentence that notes that the judge offered a humane ruling, which demonstrated the 'human dimension' of his judgment. In this case, humanity is invoked as the basis for going astray, for moving beyond the rule of law.

This brings us to the role of regulations and the supervision of compliance with those regulations. With relation to FinTech, how are we to imagine the work of the regulator? What shape will it take? Will the regulator only look at outcomes, or will they check the code line by line? Or alternatively: will the regulator deploy their own algorithm to monitor the algorithms used by FinTech companies?

We must also ask if the regulator will be up to the task in general. The current backlog in policing cybercrime seems to indicate that when it comes to containing malicious activity found in code and algorithm, the authorities are playing catch-up. This does weaken optimism for the future when it comes to FinTech compliance supervision. We must also acknowledge that the challenge in this particular case is more complex because we are not faced with a simple question of having sufficient manpower and/or skills. If the focus would only be on these two (albeit important) factors, we would bypass a much more fundamental question: is there a shared understanding of what the supervisor should be looking for? And if this question is combined with our earlier proposition of a monitoring algorithm, an additional query presents itself: can everything be coded for? In addition, how does this connect to the ideas that effective supervision must operate on the basis of principles rather than rules?

With regard to the question of whether everything can be included in an algorithm, the words of former Chief Rabbi Jonathan Sacks spring to mind. Sacks (2002) once noted that it is impossible to code for forgiveness. Forgiveness is completely irrational and utterly unpredictable – yet on the other hand, it is very understandable. This assumed impossibility of coding for forgiveness might seem to indicate some limitations of what can be included in an algorithm. An alternative lesson, however, can also be drawn. During a recent discussion on precisely this topic, someone provocatively remarked that the impossibility of coding for forgiveness should not be seen as a limitation on artificial intelligence, but rather as an indication of the end to forgiveness. Time will no doubt ultimately tell, but perhaps it is good to reaffirm that we need not be bystanders in this debate.

Concluding remarks

The possibilities of FinTech seem endless. Generally, this has very positive connotations. However, I believe the introduction of morality to the overall debate on FinTech should take place right now – before the oncoming major developments in the field, and not as an after-thought. What can we expect from FinTech? How should it be allowed to achieve its goal? How do we ensure that FinTech remains 'connected' to society? These and many more normative questions need to be fed into the debate on FinTech – a debate that currently focuses far too much on technicalities.

In short, we need to think about and discuss questions of ethics in relation to FinTech. There is a clear need to do so, especially now that we still have the opportunity to do it. If we miss this opportunity, FinTech could very well become our new Waterloo.

1. Interestingly enough, this way of using 'Waterloo' was in use long before pop group ABBA immortalised the phenomenon in their eponymously titled song. A much earlier example can be found in Sir Arthur Conan Doyle's The Return of Sherlock Holmes (2011; first published 1905).

Bibliography

Doyle, Arthur Conan. *The Return of Sherlock Holmes.* London: Penguin, 2011.

Sacks, J. *The Dignity of Difference. How to Avoid the Clash of Civilisations.* London and New York: Continuum Books, 2002.

A European Response to Digitalisation and Globalisation

By Haroon Sheikh

THE DUTCH ECONOMY is doing well. Growth has increased, government finances are healthy and the position of the consumer is improving. The economy of the Netherlands is once again among the fastest growing economies in Europe. Finally, after years of crisis, the Dutch financial sector is doing well.

Yet this is not the moment to lean back in satisfaction. It remains a valid question whether the underlying problems of the previous crisis, such as excessive levels of debt, have been resolved adequately. More important are two substantial global developments that can have a disruptive future effect on our economy and the financial sector in particular: digitalisation and new global relations. Both indicate a radical reorientation of the relationship between society and the financial sector. To guide that reorientation, (Western) Europe can draw inspiration from the tradition of the Rhineland model, provided that we manage to renew this model in accordance with contemporary realities.

The digitalisation of reality

The influence of digitalisation can be felt everywhere in daily life and has an ever greater impact on the domain of finance. The sector itself is in fact no stranger to practices of digitalisation. For decades, banks have relied on mainframes and software to store and manage their data. This has led the banks to encounter the handicap of a head start. Through the years, financial institutions have constructed layers of software. The result is a spaghetti of IT-systems that are hard to replace, inefficient, and extremely costly to maintain. Large banks pay hundreds of millions of euros per year to maintain *legacy*-systems. This creates a space for innovative start-ups to disrupt the playing field. Using new technologies, they can offer financial products at a much lower price. Furthermore, the new European PSD2-law obliges banks to allow their consumers the space to share financial data with third parties. This creates further opportunities

162

for new players in the field.

The real threat is not posed by the large number of small new companies, but by the small number of technological giants that have now reached immense proportions. These are sometimes referred to as *the frightful five*. Apple has a market value that exceeds the Dutch GDP; Facebook has more users than China has citizens. And these companies are gradually expanding to other sectors, among them the retail industry and healthcare. What fuels this sectoral expansion and how can we understand the disruptive power of the internet? To understand this, we have to consider two things: the business model of the internet and the nature of the global digital infrastructure that is currently being constructed.

Traditional companies in the pre-Internet era experienced the real problem of managing their supply in accordance with demand on the market. Large organisations were necessary to centralise supply in an efficient manner, including: journalists working for a newspaper, TV programmes, and food products in a supermarket. Successful companies were industry specialists at distributing their combined supply to customers. The logistics chain was the core of the process; from there, these companies could focus on the consumer.

The main difference with the internet is that supply distribution has become much less complex. It is virtually free to distribute news, videos, and music through the internet. The marginal costs are also non-existent; as soon as an app reaches the App Store, there is no additional cost to obtaining several million users of that app. There is a world of difference with the extremely costly processes involved in the logistic chains of the past. This is why internet platforms pursue a different business model. Rather than aggregating and distributing their supply, these companies activate consumers. Two principles are central to this approach. (1) A simple and intuitive interface. Think of the user experience of Netflix, Uber, Facebook and Booking.com, all of which are extremely user-friendly. If we contrast this with the use of services offered by utility companies, TV stations and banks, it becomes clear that they operate in a vastly different manner. (2) Intelligent systems that provide personalised recommendations based on data. This data is gathered by use of 'likes', reviews or other user data provided unconsciously. Based on this data you receive reliable taxis nearby; hotels that suit your lifestyle; and news and films that spark your interest. This principle, too, is missing in traditional companies, focused as they are on supply and distribution. In the traditional model, consumer engagement ends when the consumer leaves the store; meanwhile, internet platforms continue to gather data.

This discrepancy found in the model of supply and demand means that the impact of digitalisation on various sectors is incredibly disruptive. Already the music, newspaper, TV and travel industries have felt this disruption; meanwhile, FinTech promises to wreak similar havoc in the world of financial services. The combination of a good interface with a data-driven approach has sprouted here and there in the financial sector. Think for instance of mobile payments, the use of online wallets, and cryptocurrencies. But how can we classify the multitude of digital financial initiatives? For this, we must delve deeper into the logic of digitalisation.

An interesting point of departure for this is *The Stack*, a book by Benjamin Bratton (2016). A *stack* is a common term for the accumulation of a large number of digital products. It is a 'stack' of hardware, software and network technologies; layers that together form a particular technology. The concept of stack is used by Bratton as a metaphor for the current change taking place everywhere in reality. Instead of a 'horizontal' world of people, objects and their relations, a 'vertical', stacked structure develops. Different layers of technology together create a kind of accidental supercomputer that encompasses all of reality. Layers of that supercomputer are, for instance, atoms (energy, computable matter), hardware (devices), networks and communication (cloud services), data, sensors (in homes, cars and infrastructure), interfaces and intelligence (AI). The challenges of the future will be related to the control of different layers as well as the 'supercomputer' as a whole. This challenge is what motivates the large tech companies. Based on this idea we can come to understand their strategy of diversification: Apple in the retail industry; Google in self-driving cars; and Amazon in healthcare.

If we wish to map the threats to the financial sector, we must perform a vertical analysis. Across which layers can disruption emerge?

Disruption will not be based in the hardware layer, because we are much more concerned with services here. At the software layer, we can consider more efficient IT-platforms for banks such as the product offered by Swiss company Temenos. The layer of network- and communications technologies concerns for instance the rise of mobile banking. Simple SMS technologies sufficed in Africa to cause a great change. In Kenya, mobile payments have become so commonplace that the central bank is now monitoring telecommunications firm Safaricom. This is because a considerable part of the national money supply moves through the platform offered by that company. In the intelligence layer we have seen the emergence of cryptocurrencies and 'smart contracts', but also of robot-advisors for investments. The data layer now offers the possibility of personal purchase, savings and investment recommendations based on a consumer's data and preferences. In the interface layer, new connections spawn between people and the web, such as the use of digital voice assistants. Examples are Amazon's Alexa and Apple's Siri. If these became new interfaces, they can become gatekeepers or even decision-makers in financial services.

Using the idea of the *stack*, we can understand the emerging vertical order to which everyone must relate, financial parties included. This is a massive change; however, a second change of similar magnitude is also taking place right now.

Clash of titans

An upheaval of global relations is taking place that can be characterised as the end of the Atlantic era. This era started five hundred years ago when European countries like Portugal, Spain, the Netherlands, France, and England discovered the New World. The era culminated in twentieth-century America; the North-*Atlantic* Treaty Organisation is an expression of this. This era is now ending. A shift is taking place in which the Eurasian plain is once again becoming the centre of gravity in global relations, just as it was before the start of the Atlantic era. China has the second largest economy in the world and is constructing a new global trade network through its 'Belt and Road Initiative' (BRI) that stretches from Indonesia to Djibouti and from Pakistan to Poland. Estimates state that this range of investments, by its sheer size, is comparable to the American Marshall-plan after World War II. In this way, China is constructing a radically new economic and financial architecture. Part of this effort are new financial institutions such as the AAIB (Asian Infrastructure and Investment Bank) and the BRICS-bank. Local Chinese banks are growing fast and are obtaining an increasing international profile – this is already evident from the advertisements found in and around Schiphol Airport. In 2017, the three largest banks in the world were Chinese. The fourth largest bank was Japanese and the fifth once again Chinese. It is important to note here that the largest Chinese banks are owned by the state and as such follow state policy. Due to immense export surpluses, China also has more than three trillion US dollars in reserves, allowing them the possibility of exercising substantial influence on the financial markets.

But China is not the only rising superpower. Other countries are constructing their own regional power blocks. Over the last years, India has rivalled China as the fastest growing economy in the world; and under the guidance of Narendra Modi it has abandoned its tradition of isolationism and strengthened its international profile. Together with Japan, India is developing an alternative to China's silk road, called the 'Asian African Growth Corridor' (AAGC). Meanwhile, Russia is developing a 'Eurasian Economic Union' in the region of the former Soviet Union – a bloc of countries that are linked by the monetary system of the rouble. Turkey, gripped as it is by a Neo-Ottoman ideology, has developed imperial aspirations in the old empire; meanwhile, Iran is developing a sphere of influence in the Middle-East. There is great rivalry among these countries and their ambitions clash in several areas. Whatever happens, however, Eurasia will once again become the most dynamic region in the world, in terms of trade as well as conflict. This results in new trade and investment currents.

As national powers are developing in the East, division rules the West. Trump's *America First* policy is the most obvious example of this. He has given up the American tradition of unquestionable support to Western allies that has been the standard since World War II. Trump's movement is of a structural kind, however, and had been initiated before his inauguration. Under the Obama administration, the United States were already reducing their engagement in global conflict. In order to avoid *imperial overstretch*, America can no longer act as global law enforcement. The country is becoming more self-sufficient, for instance, through its increasing domestic energy production. Furthermore, Europe has also grown more independent in the last few years. The Eurocrisis has drawn attention back to the Union itself; and under German guidance Europe has become less oriented towards the United States. Brexit further strengthens this trend. Within the European Union, Great Britain had always been the most inclined towards the Atlantic. Now that Britain is leaving the Union, this inclination will diminish even further. A related process is the increase of scale on the political level. We could call this new scale 'continental politics'. The modern era started with city states; small urban areas with less than one million inhabitants. Venice, the Flemish Cities, Holland, and Portugal were initially the driving force of economic and political change in the world. The scale of their politics can be judged by the architectural layout of their cities. The Dam in Amsterdam or the Grote Markt in Antwerp are designed for a small group of well-to-do citizens that called the shots. The city states were replaced by nation states, chief among which were France, England and Germany. The much greater (geographical) size and larger populations of these nations states indicate that politics went through a pivotal change of scale increase. This is indicated by the size of Trafalgar Square and the Champs Élysées. These are not designed for political decision-making among the nobility, but for crowds of people that can march the wide streets in case of war. Conscription and parliamentary politics are representative of the political relations within the nation state.

The downfall of Germany and the failure of Europe in World War II marked the start of a world of continental politics. The United States and the Soviet Union are often considered nation states, but they have very different dimensions: geographically they are as big as continents, while their populations exceed a hundred million. These two superpowers cast a shadow on the once dominant European nation states. As such, Europe started its own experiment of continental politics by integrating nation states into the European Union. This effort was initially driven by crisis, but the Union is now becoming more of an autonomous entity.

In the twenty-first century, the balance is shifting in favour of continental powers across the world. China and India are no longer objects, but subjects of global politics. Russia and Brazil follow close behind. For the first time in modern history, the world is controlled by a multitude of continental powers. This results in different political dynamics: sprawling urban areas much larger than nation states; a strong intelligence apparatus to control crowds; and regional technological platforms with more than a billion users. Washington Memorial, Tiananmen Square in Beijing, and the Palace Square in St. Petersburg indicate the new dimensions of continental politics.

In this world of continental politics, the United States and China are the most influential players. Both embody very different models of society and finance. The United States champion the principle of the free market. The Trump administration has made efforts to further deregulate the financial sector. China follows a model based on state policy, in which the financial sector is guided by the government. Both models are alien to us, but considering the dynamic nature of those markets, we will have to formulate a response to them.

A European response

The Dutch economy is doing well at the moment, but the previous paragraphs are meant to indicate that we find ourselves in the calm before the storm. Two massive developments are taking place. First: the digitalisation of the economy is creating companies with disruptive business models. This also brings a different, layered architecture with it that is reorganising the entire economy. Second, we are experiencing a redistribution of power in global relations. The scale increase in politics situates us between the American market model and the Asian state model. We find that both developments have great influence on the financial sector. This period of radical change is demanding a response. Otherwise, there is a risk that the financial sector will be shaped by external influences. This means that we must formulate a role and a place for the financial sector within our society.

To achieve this, we can revert to an old tradition in continental Europe: the idea of the Rhineland model. This idea can provide guidance in the current context, though not in its original expression. We must dust off the old model and alter it to engage with contemporary challenges. If we do this, the Rhineland model can provide an inspiring and humane alternative to the dominance of markets and the state.

The Rhineland model is based on the observation that there are two different developmental models in the West: that of the Anglo-Saxon countries, such as England, America and Australia, and of the Continental countries, such as Germany, Austria, Sweden and France. Michel Albert's book *Capitalism vs. Capitalism* (1992) is generally considered one of the most important sources on the Rhineland model; though traces of this kind of thinking are already evident in Max Weber's work. Contemporary authors in the fields of 'multiple modernities' (S. N. Eisenstadt) and 'varieties of capitalism' (Hall and Soskice) build on this line of thinking.

In essence, the difference between the two models is found in the relationship with the market. Anglo-Saxon societies believe in the beneficial operation of the market and in private initiative. The invisible hand (see Adam Smith) means that private initiative benefits the public at large. The Rhineland model distrusts this kind of thinking. It states that the market fuels inequality and results in poor chances for the socially inept. In short: the market will not benefit the public at large of its own accord, but must be guided to do so by the state and civil society.

In Anglo-Saxon countries, the government is mostly concerned with the market process (that is to say: fair competition, right of access to information). Meanwhile, on the continent, governments also concern themselves with the results of the market process (who wins; who must be compensated for their losses and/or which public amenities must be in place). These are of course only ideal types, yet they reveal certain aspects of various phenomena in both types of society. Wage disparity is for instance considerably higher in Anglo-Saxon countries; and active intervention by government bodies in various sectors is a more common occurrence in continental societies. The Anglo-Saxon world relies more heavily on a *shareholder* model when organising the industry (meaning the shareholder is in charge), while in the Rhineland model the *stakeholders* are in charge (which are not only the shareholders but also employees and the society in which a business exists). Financial markets fill a different role in both models. In the Rhineland model, banks often cooperate with businesses to achieve long-term goals. In the Anglo-Saxon model, banks and businesses are rather at odds with one another, both endeavouring to achieve profit for themselves. As a result, businesses are more likely to collect funding through the stock exchange, while companies on the continent would sooner collect this money from the 'home' bank.

Now that the Anglo-Saxon countries are gradually removing themselves (politically) from the European continent, the Rhineland model is a powerful idea that can foster collaboration between countries for a European alternative. It is neither the hard market of America, nor the all-powerful state of Asia. Meanwhile the model must be adjusted to the contemporary context. For this reason, I will finish with three suggestions for that adjustment:

1) The idea of *stakeholders* is powerful, but must be defined more broadly. Historically, the emphasis has been on labour and trade unions. In the current, highly fractured labour market, many people no longer identify with these institutions. 'Stakeholders' as a concept will have to be understood more widely. We must also take into account societal norms, which have become more involved with the economy. Discussions on equality, discrimination, and sustainability are increasingly linked to production and consumption. A moralisation of economy is taking place: production must remain sustainable and companies must be accountable to the public; for instance, with regard to diversity and the way they use cheap labour. We should understand the concept of the stakeholder from this broad societal context.

2) The Rhineland model must obtain a more substantive orientation through the allocation of ambitious goals. At the moment, the model is mostly employed in a defensive way, for instance to prevent the hostile takeover of Dutch companies by American shareholders. A positive substantiation of the concept is rarely heard. If we do not come to understand the model in this way, our policy will be understood as simple protectionism. The alternative to this is to define concrete projects to which the Dutch economy dedicates itself. We could think of the question

of global food safety. This requires an alliance of large companies, universities (such as Wageningen University), the national government and citizens' associations cooperating in a common ecosystem. With such a goal and the associated ecosystem in mind, a much better argument can be made to prevent the takeover of a company like Unilever.

3) We must think about new, future-proof institutions. Contemporary capitalism moves rapidly. While ecosystems are slowly chipping away at long-term goals, mere seconds are required for monumental change on the stock markets. For this reason, we require institutions that are able to combine the logic of the markets with social well-being. A possibility would be the foundation of a Dutch *Sovereign Wealth Fund*, a state-controlled investment fund. These are not only found in oil-rich countries in the Middle East or in export-heavy Asian countries, but also in countries that are more similar to the Netherlands: Norway, Chile and Australia. Such a fund could obtain options in Dutch businesses to protect them from external parties, and subsequently invest in alliances with start-ups, governments and knowledge centres. The fund could be a propagator for the aforementioned big projects and could contribute to the long-term profitability of the Netherlands.

Technology and globalisation will cause profound changes to the Netherlands and our financial sector in the years to come. This is why it is imperative to formulate a response now. Fortunately, we can refer to our tradition of the Rhineland model, provided this model is adapted to a contemporary context.

Bibliography

Albert, Michel. *Capitalism Against Capitalism*. Hoboken, NJ: Wiley, 1992.

Bratton, Benjamin H. *The Stack. On Software and Sovereignty*. Boston, MA: MIT Press, 2016.

Finance, State, and Society in Europe

By Herman Van Rompuy

IN THIS CONTRIBUTION, I will not address the technical lessons we can draw from the decade after the financial crisis of 2008. Instead, I will focus on the kind of ideas and values we must put into practice in the future, as well as what kind of non-values we should avoid. Avoiding the worst is often 'doing the good'.

Financial markets and regulation

The banking crisis and the Eurozone crisis made it clear that we did not learn from the disastrous crisis of the 1930s. Right before the crisis, some still believed in the ideology of the self-regulation, or 'invisible hand', of the financial sector. This brought us only a few millimetres away from the total collapse of the global financial system. We require deregulation in certain sectors to foster growth and jobs; in other sectors, however, we need *more* regulation. And even today this debate is far from over. The Trump administration is once again going down the ideological path of deregulation. As a result, European bankers will exercise pressure on European lawmakers to soften their stance on regulation; all in the name of maintaining a competitive European position in the financial sector. In general, the financial markets are not perfect allocators of economic factors. Before 2010, the 'spreads' of Greek bonds were very small, as if the huge deficits on the current account of the balance of payments were not a huge problem. After 2010, however, the markets panicked and gave disproportionate weight to minor problems in some of the European member states. Financial markets are not a good guide for economic decisions. Today, bubbles in the bitcoin and equity markets demonstrate once again that nationality has disappeared. Investors anticipate the expectations of other investors. As a side note: bitcoins are no coins, but assets. Regulation is needed in this field as much as anywhere else. Finally, besides market failure we find the occurrence of political failure.

Lessons for Europe

In the 'good times' preceding the year 2008, European authorities were informed about the underlying problems in various countries of the Eurozone. They were told about real estate bubbles in some countries, about a weak EMU, and more. A change of course was discouraged, however, because it seemed there were no problems on the macro-economic front. Short-termism is a disease in politics, as it is elsewhere. The 'common good' necessitates leadership. There can be as much of a leadership deficit as there can be a democratic deficit.

One of the reasons for political failure in Europe in the years preceding 2008 was the reluctance at additional transfers of sovereignty. The EU launched a common currency, but could not decide on common policies and common institutions. Only a crisis – a lasting crisis – changed this deadlock.

Even today, the argument for national sovereignty is used as a decisive one. It is presented as a red line. But the EU, from the very start, has always been an enterprise of transferring sovereignty, or of shared sovereignty. Another unavoidable reality, one that was only acknowledged after the crisis struck, is that each country in a monetary union is *responsible for the whole*. Misgovernment at the national level has consequences for all other members of the Union. Those who made mistakes have to adjust. Meanwhile, solidarity is needed to help countries with problems in overcoming them. Solidarity is needed in a common enterprise, alongside responsibility. We require both risk-sharing and risk-reducing. This is the basis of every compromise, at any level of governance.

It took years before people finally realised that a Union is more than the sum of its member states. Some thought that if every member state would see to their own affairs properly, the Eurozone as a whole would function well. However, there was also a systemic, transversal, specific European dimension to the financial crisis. This became clear when the EC decided on a single supervisor for all banks in the Eurozone. The turning point in the crisis came in the summer of 2012. This was the moment we decided on this mega-reform. Indeed, the whole is more than the sum of its parts. Of course, the Banking Union constitutes a transfer of sovereignty as well as a further step in expanding the EMU. Ignoring this constitutes a rearguard action.

My position in this debate is not inspired by an ideological drive towards 'more Europe'. It is simply the logical conclusion of decisions codified in the 1992 Maastricht Treaty. It is a matter of coherence much more than one of simple conviction. Euroscepticism and all kinds of semi- or outright populism prevent leaders from looking ahead in time and perceiving the common good and the longer term. I would like to add that in the end, we overcame the existential crisis of the Eurozone precisely because we put aside all these prejudices. My point here is that this process took time, and that we should not make the same mistakes in the future.

A long and winding road

The challenge now is to decide on a stronger Eurozone (and a stronger Schengen area) outside the context of a crisis. How do we convince leaders that we must anticipate? One day – hopefully a long time from now – there will be a new financial or migration crisis. Are we ready to face such a crisis? We know what to do with regards to the EMU. Reports by four or five presidents of EU institutions indicate the way. New proposals by the Commission, along with the ideas of President Macron and fourteen leading economists, are extremely helpful. But the question remains: who will lead us? I believe it can only be France and Germany. They are, respectively, sensitive to solidarity and to responsibility. This is not a matter of re-inventing the EU; it is a matter of re-energising it.

Naturally, we need all member states on board in this process. Leadership is required, however – especially in times of populism and the re-emergence of nationalist feelings.

Already, I notice in some member states a feeling of unease about a possible Franco-German initiative. Who else will do the job though? Neither a standstill nor cosmetic reforms are feasible alternatives. This should not be a time of narrow-mindedness, but of a broader and longer-term view. The Union seems to be used to making hard decisions only in times of crisis. But we must do it differently this time: we have to act in economically stable times. We must 'make the Union great again' – though in a constructive and positive way, far from aggression and negative feelings like revenge, nostalgia, conflict, anger, and jealousy.

This exercise of 'relaunching' the European project should not be restricted to a series of technical reforms. We have to touch upon the 'heart' of the matter. What do I mean by that? At all levels, we must reconcile openness with protection. We need open economies with free and fair trade, parallel to the free movement of goods, services, people, and capital. We require open societies, ones that accept minorities in a tolerant way and integrate newcomers whilst safeguarding the borders. We need open democracies with due respect for pluralism and the rule of law, including within the Union; with respect for gender equality, the separation of Church and State, and the freedom of speech and religion. And we need protection against unemployment; insecure jobs; huge inequalities; climate change; uncontrolled migration; social-, commercial- and tax dumping; terrorism and violence, corruption and fraud. If people do not feel well-protected, they pursue protectionism, tribalism, and nationalism. Every state has to protect its people, without folding back on itself. We have to create a space and a place. We have to reconcile the web-people and the wall-people, the movers and those who stay at home, those from nowhere and those from somewhere.

If that message cannot be conveyed, the Franco-German initiative and the European Council will have failed. The answer to many of these challenges will be increased European cooperation and more integration, not less. This should be understood as the result of the search for a compromise between openness and protection. It is *not* an a priori position of pro-Europeans.

I repeat, this balance must be found at the national as well as at the regional level. Consider the case of the United States. They face the same kind of problems Europe does, such as migration, terrorism, inequality, free and fair trade, job insecurity, et cetera. The current answer in the US is a populist one: closing off the country rather than opening it up. And yet America was great *precisely when it was open*. This is the true paradox. There are, of course, differences between the US and the EU. A qualitative difference is the high degree of income inequality in the US, which has dramatically increased since the '80s. Wages are lagging behind productivity. The same trend of rising inequality is found in Russia and China, but it does not exist in the EU – at least not in our member states. There are a few exceptions to this rule, especially in member states where unemployment has risen considerably during the Eurozone crisis. In Western Europe, populism has risen in response to uncontrolled migration. In Southern Europe, it is on the rise because of unemployment; and in the Anglo-Saxon world, it protests inequality.

A *word on populism*

Populism can influence economic conditions in different ways and via different channels. Populist parties everywhere in Europe are on the political right side when it comes to migration and identity issues, but on the defensive side regarding socio-economic matters. With regard to the latter, they are opposed to structural reforms and to fiscal consolidation. Meanwhile, populism contributes to the fragmentation of the political landscape. At the moment, the EU has several countries run by minority governments. This makes it much more difficult to achieve a stable and long-term policy. And populist parties are by nature anti-European, though they appear to accept more and more the fact that the European Union exists. Why is this? Because after Brexit, Trump, and Putin, Europeans firmly oppose any type of exit. Populists want to remain popular and so they bend to the will of the people. But they will never deepen or strengthen the Union. They will not leave the EU due to their voters, but 'more Europe' is never on the agenda. This approach leads to a weaker Europe, a more fragile Eurozone, and a less pronounced role in the world.

Meanwhile, mainstream parties are tempted to partially copy the rhetoric of populists. Some do this in order to cushion excesses, but most do it for opportunistic reasons. This makes the victory of President Macron so interesting. He did not give in to populist rhetoric or policies.

In some countries, mainstream and populist parties are converging. The former adopt more right-wing stances on migration, while the latter become more 'European'. Populism is the result of evolutions in our societies. It can be combated politically, but for this our societies must first become more balanced and more just.

The new European programme

What should be the content of the new European programme? It has to be focused on three objectives: prosperity, security and fairness. Let me shortly elaborate on each one of them.

Prosperity
Both the EU and the US need a higher productivity growth through increased private and public investments. To improve the business climate is first and foremost a job for the individual member states. Improvements must go beyond lowering corporate taxes, as this can end in worldwide fiscal competition. The investments have to do with financial capital (venture capital; the Capital Markets Union), human capital (education; the 'war on talents') and physical capital. When we look at the European level, the 'Investment Plan for Europe' (or the 'Juncker Plan') must become permanent. Until 2020, it triggers a total of 500 billion euros, or more than 3% of the GDP. Our common, ambitious climate policy is an incentive for massive investments in renewable energy.

I also believe that the EU-budget for 2020-2027 should focus on merit-based Research and Design, and on joint efforts in future-oriented activities. The European Union's Horizon 2020 programme is the biggest scientific programme in the world.

Prosperity demands a further deepening of our single market (the digital, energy, and services aspects of it, at a public as well as a private level). This has a high potential for productivity gains. It is certainly a work in progress, but I believe it is developing too slowly.

A 'genuine' EMU would lead to a completion of the Banking Union, a Fiscal Union (with an adapted Stability and Growth pact) and an Economic Union (with efforts towards economic reforms and towards more convergence – after all, a common policy needs more common policies). We are aware that gradualism is inevitable, but the first new steps have to be taken immediately. Postponing them would undermine the Union's credibility once again.

A financial crisis in the future is a real possibility. The Euro area and the Schengen zone were designed for normal, stable times. They were not designed to face the biggest financial crisis since the thirties, nor for facing the biggest influx of migrants from outside the Union ever. We must anticipate future crises. However, to decide on reforms without being with our 'backs against the wall' requires leadership.

In each and every proposal, we will have to overcome at least two taboos: the transfer of sovereignty, and an increase in solidarity. If we do not overcome these taboos, our efforts will only result in symbols of a 'Minister of Finance' and a 'European Monetary Fund'.

Our prosperity also depends on open markets, both inside and outside the European Union. The FTA agenda of the Commission is huge: on the to-do list are India, Mercosur, Australia, New Zealand, and Indonesia.

Meanwhile, the EU is still in a process of enlargement - we are negotiating with Serbia and Montenegro. Croatia became a member of the Union in 2013. There is less enlargement fatigue in the Union than most politicians seem to think.

Finally, a note on employment. This is to a large extent a national competence. A new balance must be found between flexibility (which in some countries is too high, resulting in social 'malaise') and security (which often results in too much rigidity).

Security
The European Union must promote legal migration and actively combat illegal entries. Only when we can control illegal migration will we be able to garner enough public support for the inevitably needed legal migration (if only for demographic reasons). We also require a more common asylum and migration policy. Meanwhile, we must protect our external borders in order to be able to maintain the passport-free zone, as we did until now. This should be done in cooperation with riparian countries. Finally, we must fight and eradicate terrorism through more integrated policies and agencies.

The EU should endeavour to help develop Africa, a continent of demographic revolution and huge migration potential.

A military dimension of the Union should be developed by spending more and spending better. Cooperation is required between armies and industries; to this end, we can employ economies of scale while avoiding fragmentation. We must make European 'battle groups' operational. Interesting steps have already been taken in recent months, ahead of the formal debate on the 'future of Europe', such as a unified command of EU crisis operations and permanent structured cooperation (PESCO).

Fairness
Fairness is first and foremost a national competence. The EU can contribute (and has been doing so, in fact, since 2013) by combating international tax fraud and evasion, by fighting against other types of dumping (such as social and commercial), and by tackling discrimination between SMEs and multinational corporations. A country by itself can have no impact on international and/or global evolutions. Only a bloc like the EU has enough leverage to correct market distortions.

Resistance to the objectives
The three objectives outlined above are meeting deep-rooted frustrations and desires among citizens of EU member states. Accomplishing these objectives must be a joint effort by the 27 member states. However, some member states are already more integrated than others (think of the Eurozone; Schengen). Countries should not hinder others to integrate further and in more domains. The instruments for this purpose are foreseen in the Treaties: enhanced cooperation and PESCO. In any case, every individual member state must have the possibility to join the vanguard at a later time.

The 'leaders' agenda' will require leadership

It requires a sense of compromise to tackle the challenges I have outlined. We need to balance responsibility and solidarity, security and solidarity, national sovereignty and integration, and growth and cohesion. We always require both parts. One cannot applaud with one hand. If we cannot combine solidarity with security and responsibility, we will fail to find an agreement between North and South on future EMU reforms, and between West and East on the migration challenge. Tensions can be surmounted, on one condition: we need to have the political will and leadership to overcome them. Only then will we obtain win-win solutions.

The European Council has agreed on a 'leaders' agenda', a timetable of eighteen months to make decisions in specific domains. But we should never lose sight of the bigger picture. Our citizens need to be able to see what the purpose of this exercise is. They must feel that their concerns are being taken seriously. The 'leaders' agenda' is very ambitious. This 'leaders' agenda' will need leadership. The 'window of opportunity' is small both in size and time – we must take into account the European elections in June 2019.

Defeating populism is not an aim in itself. It is the result of positive action, to better protect our citizens against threats whilst keeping our democracies, our economies, and our societies open. The defeat of populism is a 'collateral benefit' of that action. 'Plus est en vous' ('More in you') should be the slogan for a programme of re-energising Europe.

The Global Agenda, the New Economy, and Integrity: Towards a Sustainable Financial Sector

By Jan Peter Balkenende

THE 2008 FINANCIAL crisis has served as a wake-up call. We see a growing number of companies that are committed to integrating Corporate Social Responsibility (CSR) and sustainability principles into their business models. The emerging Global Agenda has not gone unnoticed in the financial sector and serious efforts are being made to address the Sustainable Development Goals and the challenges posed by the Circular or New Economy. For many, the question has become: 'How can we do business while contributing to human flourishing, a living planet, and a vital society?'

At the same time, we recognise that old habits, structures and interests are strong and that the possibility of a return to 'business as usual' in the banking sector is ever present. That would be dangerous, if only because there is still a lot of public discontent and distrust about the economy, and the financial sector in particular. This dates from the 2008 crisis and even before. As Dirk Bezemer and Govert Buijs note earlier in this volume, populism feeds on this distrust and resentment, which again is reinforced by the fact that the mechanisms of the financial system are widening the income and wealth inequality gaps.

This is our challenge: how can we harness and strengthen positive changes in the sector? And which other initiatives should be part of an effective and inspiring, inclusive, and future-oriented agenda, that takes into account the revolutionary developments in technology, corporate organisation and geopolitics that mark the current era?

It is my strong conviction that we need to bring values and purpose into the equation. I think we will not bring about sustained change in the policies of companies, the financial sector, and the economy if this change is not accompanied by and built on a strong ethic of inclusiveness at all levels.

But how? Setting the agenda

A crucial issue is of course *education*: to bring about change in our schools and universities in the very first place. What are the ethical perspectives that are transmitted through our curricula? What are the starting points, what are the roots of our thinking? Is education merely about 'what' we do and 'how' we do it, i.e. about goals and strategy? Should it obfuscate the 'why' of what we do, the purpose?

It all starts with the conviction that we need to think differently. Fortunately, there are already initiatives of this kind. See for example the work of Lans Bovenberg, earlier in this volume: he is doing a great job by working on changing the mainstream curriculum for economics education with his relational view on the economy. It is imperative that we encourage a conversation on values and purpose in schools and universities.

When it comes to changing mind-sets, I believe that good *leadership* can make a difference. I refer to leadership in tandem with exemplary behaviour: to live up to the vision that our efforts are not about 'me, now', but about 'we, tomorrow'. We need to promote values-based leadership and management, based on an awareness of every person's and each company's responsibilities in and to society. I notice a positive trend in this respect. More and more captains of industry are motivated by a reflection on what is and what will be their legacy, their contribution beyond having served self-interest and the immediate interests of the company. What is their meaning for other people, society, the planet?

I would also like to point to the fact that the SDG's – Sustainable Development Goals - have an important and inspiring mobilising potential. In the international sphere, the SDG's have thus far received considerable attention, and it is important to connect to and capitalise on this movement.

Finally, there is a growing body of new insights and initiatives that feed this movement for change. Here, I may refer to - for example - the Caux Round Table and the Moral Capitalism initiative, presided by Stephen Young (cf. 2003), and to the Conscious Capitalism initiative, led by Raj Sisodia (cf. Mackey and Sisodia 2013). The plea for Inclusive

Capitalism by Acemoğlu and Robinson in their insightful book *Why nations fail* (2014) is considered more relevant than ever. The success of Kate Raworth's *Doughnut Economics* (2017) further testifies to the broadly shared impetus for change.

The need for a dialogue between the financial sector, business, government and society

Unfortunately, I do not think that education and the promotion of values-based leadership will suffice. Sylvester Eijffinger, member of the 'Maas' Commission on banking, reminds us in his contribution that it is hard to tame the risk appetite of managers when stakes are high. In the end, Eijffinger says, the quality of any risk management system, or of governance in general, depends on immaterial factors such as character. Can we select on character? And how do we maintain an ethical perspective over time? There is no alternative but to organise a recurrent and meaningful dialogue on personal and business ethics.

We can probably find a clue in the contribution of Theodor Kockelkoren. While conceding that a clear regulatory framework is essential for the proper functioning of financial institutions, he points at the limits of regulation and the counterproductive effects of ever more detailed regulation. As an alternative, Kockelkoren proposes to enter into dialogue with financial institutions on what would be the ideals, values and purposes underlying laws that govern the regulatory framework. An agreement and ongoing dialogue at the level of principle then leaves ample discretionary space for practical implementation by financial institutions themselves.

In this way, not only do we improve the quality of services rendered by financial institutions, we also come closer to the societal purpose that is embodied in regulatory laws. At least as important, however, is the fact that something unique is happening here: people – both regulators and bankers, and those working in other financial institutions – are having a dialogue on ethical perspectives and their practical consequences. They are learning to think inclusively; they are changing their mind-set; and they are enriching their ethical perspectives. Ultimately, all that will be the best guarantee for sustainable change.

Dialogue on values and purpose in an interconnected world

In an interconnected world, no single actor – be they a bank, company, or country – can bring about fundamental change. Nor can they change themselves without risking their very existence. Change can only be the outcome of agreements and commitments by the collective of decisive stakeholders, agreed upon in an ongoing conversation, in which together they enact or generate a shared purpose. Only if decisive stakeholders cooperate and coordinate their efforts can change be possible. This requires dialogue, because in dialogue we can generate the mind-set and trust that is needed to come to mutual commitments in collective efforts. I believe this is the fundamental insight that guides the Socires programme.

Furthermore, for change to be feasible and sustainable, the initiative should operate on a significant scale. What comes to mind is the *European level*, and in particular the countries which feature the social market economy or the Rhineland model. Though it has suffered from Anglo-Saxon influences, the idea of coordinated efforts between different stakeholders remains key.

Is there room for a particular, relatively autonomous and proper European arrangement in the global financial environment? Yes, but it can only be the result of mutual commitment and trust. It cannot exist as a separatist movement. It is time to create a new European dream. How do we bring this idea of a strong, European movement from head to heart and hands? Internationally, there is still considerable admiration for the European project. The revitalisation of the European idea – starting in the financial sector – can make the EU a moral world leader.

Bibliography

Acemoğlu, Daron, and James Robinson. *Why Nations Fail - The Origins of Power, Prosperity, and Poverty.* New York: Crown Publishing, 2014.

Mackey, John, and Raj Sisodia. *Conscious Capitalism - Liberating the Heroic Spirit of Business.* Boston: Harvard Business Review Press, 2013.

Raworth, Kate. *Doughnut Economics - Seven Ways to Think Like a 21st-Century Economist.* New York: Random House Business, 2017.

Young, Stephen. *Moral Capitalism - Reconciling Private Interest with the Public Good.* Oakland, CA: Berrett-Koehler Publishers, 2003.

Fintech and the Common Good

By Rens van Tilburg

Socires and the Sustainable Finance Lab (SFL) each followed their own trajectory in discovering how finance should be transformed in order to serve the common good. The coming years we will cooperate in the program Finance and the Common Good, aimed at developing a Rhineland 'way of finance'. In this, SFL will focus on the application of new technologies. I hereby describe my introduction to Socires at the 2018 Rhineland Economic Forum. After that I introduce the ideas SFL will be working on, how new technologies can allow people to express their social and ecological values also in their financial activities.

The Rhineland Economic Forum

On January 23 2018, the global elite gathered in Davos, Switzerland, to discuss the Great Issues of our times. On that same day, a gathering of considerable power and influence also took place in the Netherlands. At the Vrije Universiteit Amsterdam, located at the national business centre, the Zuidas, former Christian-Democratic prime minister Jan Peter Balkenende and his Minister of Finance Wouter Bos of the Social-Democrats shared the stage. This was the first time they were together on a public stage since their years in the cabinet that steered the Netherlands through the crisis years following the fall of Lehman brothers. Former EU Council President Herman Van Rompuy made his appearance, as did Carla Moonen, then chairwoman of the Pension Fund for Care and Well-Being (PFZW), the second largest pension fund of the Netherlands with over 200 billion euros in pension savings. The current Minister of Finance, Wopke Hoekstra, called on the bankers, entrepreneurs and politicians present to go beyond their individual responsibilities and tasks and to focus on their shared responsibility for the well-being and resilience of society as a whole.

This conference was the apotheosis of the "Ethics and Finance" trajectory of Socires, a think tank founded by former Christian

Democratic senator Jos van Gennip. Those present - leaders and thinkers from within and around the financial sector debated "The Finance-State-Society Triangle in Europe; the past and the next forty years". No light fare, but food for wide-ranging reflections and fundamental discussions by an extremely varied company: from fairly young to very old, from political left to right, from scientists to bankers and from Dutch to Belgians, French and Germans.

Earlier sessions with exclusively Dutch participants had concluded that there are still many fundamental issues in and around the financial sector needing resolution. However financiers cannot find and implement the needed solutions themselves, nor can politicians impose them. The problems are too fundamental, too complex. What is needed is a coordinated interplay between state, society and the financial sector. And not just in the Netherlands, but on the broader stage - where business and finance operate and where political decisions are increasingly made.

We are the problem

Former Minister of Finance, Wouter Bos quoted his response back then - during a popular Dutch TV-show. When asked about what caused the crisis, and tired of blaming bankers, their bonuses and the system that let them get away with it all, he replied to the question who is to blame: "all of us (..) who always want more, more, more". Founded in our "consumption mentality" a system was built that allowed risk taking and greed to attain unsustainable levels.

Bos seldom received more criticism, but rarely was he more right. And that is the dilemma of those in leading positions. As then euro President, Jean-Claude Juncker once said: "Politicians know very well what needs to be done to resolve the euro crisis. The problem is that they do not know how they can be re-elected after they have done this." For bankers a similar logic applies. Former Rabobank board member Rien Nagel recalled how before the crisis over-crediting was the norm: every bank had to participate, had to follow suit to keep its market share and to stay in business. One had to move with the herd. With rising levels of loan-to-value (in the Netherlands mortgage loans reached 130% of home values, where 80% is the maximum in most countries) this increasingly felt like "running towards the abyss with the herd".

That has not changed. With short-term horizons and herd behavior, politicians and financiers both still feel the pressure. But the problem is not limited to these two professions. Former EU Council president Herman Van Rompuy pointed to the rot elsewhere in society, from sex scandals in the church to doping in sports.

Renewal requires a new dialogue ...

The necessary renewal of the financial sector requires an interplay between state, society and financial sector. It starts with a widely shared, clear problem analysis. We must break through the mesmerizing formulas that now color the official discourse, where problems are clouded rather than named: As if we have solved the eurocrisis in a way that will prevent it from recurring. As if we have advanced from a 'bail-out' financial sector to 'bail-in' where tax payers' money will no longer be needed to fill the holes after financial bets have turned sour. "Fake news!" According to the eminent German economist Martin Hellwig.

We need to confront questions like: How is the way we have organized the financial-monetary system connected with the major problems of our time such as climate change, social inequality, uncertainty and distrust? How are the state, society and financial sector connected to each other? Which "structures of sin" (in the words of professor Paul Dembinski of Switzerland's Fribourg University) have we built? Dutch journalist, academic and bank regulator Christiaan Vos pointed to the shift in the zeitgeist than can be distilled from the two 'Wall Street' films starring Michael Douglas as the greedy investment banker Gordon Gekko. It went from bad to worse. In 1987, Gordon Gekko told his apprentice "Greed is good". This motto allowed Gekko to become rich, but he ended up behind bars. In the sequel in 2010, things were much better for the banker. Greed was no longer considered just good, Gekko could now declare "Greed is legal!".

A clear direction for the financial sector emerged from the presentations and discussions at the conference. A shift is needed on several dimensions: from transactions to relationships, from long chains of anonymous actors to direct relationships between people, from complexity to transparency and simplicity. These are still rather abstract notions, but they give direction to a new relationship between state, society and financial sector.

We seek a new relationship in which citizens are emancipated and transcend the dominance of state and market, in which employees claim their right to make ethical choices also at their workplaces, where shoppers in the supermarket overcome the consumer in themselves, where we leave the realm of scarcity - the country where economists feel so at home, and start to realize how abundantly many of our needs are already fulfilled.

That future is already with us, argued Carla Moonen, of the Pension Fund for Care and Well-Being (PFZW). The nurses and care-givers she talks to ask her to go beyond maximizing financial return. Their desire to care for the world extends to the way their pensions - their largest personal savings - are invested.

How to combine required financial returns with socially desirable development within sustainable ecological boundaries? How do these reinforce each other and where do trade-offs need to be made? And if so, how do we make these trade-offs? How should the financial sector re-invent itself to achieve these goals? Who should be involved in addressing these questions and how? These are the questions that we of the Sustainable Finance Lab (SFL) will explore with Socires in our new three year program 'Finance and the Comon Good'. A program that we will execute with leading thinkers and practitioners, from finance, academia and the public sector. The necessary renewal requires a delicate and inspired interplay between state, society and the financial sector; the domains that now point the finger at each other for the problems at hand. A start is to restore the relationship between these domains. This requires commitment from engaged thinkers and do-ers: an open dialogue in an environment that transcends polarized dominance of state and market, insight into each other's situation, motives and possibilities. Only in such a relational environment, from proximity rather than distance, from rela-tionship rather than transaction, can sustainable social and ecological recovery be achieved.

Such a development only has winners. Good financial returns cannot be sustained in a world with excessive social and ecological tensions. The idea that there is an inherent trade-off between financial return and positive social and ecological impact has been falsified by hundreds of studies. Where this trade-off does exist, it is by no means evident that the financial return should trump other concerns. Retired people want to enjoy a good pension, in a healthy environment. And a financial sector that visibly contributes to human values while preserving nature will certainly also benefit the well-being of everyone working in this sector. It will ensure that they can tell proud stories to their children and at birthday parties about where they spend most of their time and talents on. Stories about why they do this and with what results, not just for the financial bottom line, but for the planet and its people.

... at a Rhineland level

Action is needed at a scale that goes well beyond the Netherlands. A fruitful scale is the Rhineland: the Benelux, France and Germany. Austria, Switzerland and Northern Italy can also be added. These are countries and regions that share a long history, a common culture and where the free market has never been the sole touchstone of wisdom, where there is a common understanding that life is about more than making money, and that the role of the state encompasses more than just repairing market failures. Here there is a tradition of a self-organizing society, of cooperatives and commons based cooperation amongst citizens. The world's largest cooperatives are situated in the Rhineland, and what's more, in the financial sector: Groupe Credit Agricole and Groupe Bank Populaire Caisse d'Epargne (BPCE) in France and the Bundesverband der Deutschen Volksbanken und Raiffeisenbanken (BVR) in Germany.[1] The Dutch financial sector too has large cooperatives, with Rabobank in banking and Achmea in insurance.

The Rhineland is the birthplace and the heartland of the social-market economy - a model that before 2008 was quickly losing ground. Since then, there is a clear Renaissance of this thinking, although it is still uncertain where this will lead.

A great deal could be gained by a comparison across these countries of the domains of state, finance, business, academia and society. And a comparison to the Anglo-Saxon formula that we have tested over the past 40 years and that has failed to deliver on its promise. It is time to renounce our belief in an invisible hand, and put our trust in our own hands - in what they together can deliver. With Brexit at hand and Trump in the White House, there is no better time to look to the Rhineland for inspiration and cooperation. What inspiration can we now derive from the age-old social market and cooperative tradition that characterizes these countries? We seek a dialogue with our closest (literally and figuratively) neighbours.

All the while we should not disregard the many interesting developments in Scandinavian countries. Nor the alternatives developed in the UK and the US, as it is here that the drawbacks of the free market revolution have been felt early and most strongly, stimulating the formulation of clear alternatives.

Value based financial technology

The shared ambition of Socires and the SFL is to develop a common understanding of the need for and direction of renewal in the way society organizes its financial functions, as well as to help kick-start some very practical renewals. Our aim is to change how we manage our finance, how we save, how we allocate funds to entrepreneurs who not only realize an adequate financial return, but that also best realize the social and ecological values that owners of capital deem most valuable.

This is not an exercise in recreating a lost financial sector. Rather it is about enabling today's citizens to let their money work in line with their deepest held convictions - using the new possibilities that technologies offer. New technologies that provide possibilities that were unimaginable until very recently.

So how can these new technologies give rise to a Rhineland model of finance? How can they help materialize the shift in finance from transactions to relationships, from long chains of anonymous actors to direct relationships between people, from complexity to transparency and simplicity? Let us illustrate this with a few examples.

Crowdfunding as Value-based Finance

Banks play a dominant role in the Rhineland financial sector. Historically banks have been relational institutions par excellence. It was through their many, deep and long standing relationships with entrepreneurs that they knew best where credit was due. Through recent decades banks have to a large extent lost this role. Banks have become more transaction oriented, making mortgage and collateral lending a much larger part of their business as opposed to lending based on an analysis of the individual entrepreneur and market opportunities. We do see banks trying to reverse this trend. They struggle, however, at the same time with the increasingly high cost of real economy lending and with a regulatory framework that has adapted to transaction-banking, thus further entrenching this mode of operation, making it the new norm.

For these reasons a host of alternative finance institutions has emerged since 2008. They try to fill the gap banks left in funding Small and Medium-sized Enterprises (SME's). One fast growing alternative is crowd-funding, a technique enabled by new information and communication technologies. Here it is lenders themselves who decide on the direction their money takes. It is their knowledge and relationships that enable the allocation of their money. As they themselves are in control, they can also take other values into account not just the financial return. The PhD research of SFL associate Helen Toxopeus (Utrecht University) on finance for sustainable innovation, shows that crowdfunder decision-making indeed takes into account multiple values, including societal impact.[2]

New technologies, through crowdfunding, thus open up possibilities for citizens to better align the way their money is invested with their values. The story does not end here. Increasingly institutional investors seek to use this 'wisdom of the crowd', putting their money in an automated way where the crowd is going, investing in companies that exceed a certain threshold of funding by the crowd. For institutional investors this is a way to reduce research costs, to invest in small companies that have previously been beyond their reach. They are no longer limited to participating in the finance of regular banks or expensive private equity. This new symbiosis between the crowd and institutional investors runs both ways, with the crowd taking into account also the analysis of institutional investors and traditional banks.[3]

The Circular Service Platform

SFL-researcher Elisa Achterberg piloted a new payment platform that facilitates the upscaling of circular business models and offers investors new ways of financing the circular economy, bypassing traditional financial intermediaries and creating the possibility of a new circular asset class that lowers financing costs for circular entrepreneurs.[4]

In a circular economy, responsibility for product performance and materials shift from end-users to all stakeholders involved in keeping an asset functioning. This comes down to providing services, (rather than selling assets) collectively, by circular supply chain networks.

The success of circular service networks relies on long-term agreements, cooperation and trust between the network participants. This comes with high transaction costs and a diametrically opposed business logic then we are used to. In a Community of Practice, an interdisciplinary open learning space, consisting of Rabobank, Allen & Overy, ABN Amro, De Lage Landen, ING, Leystromen and Bundles, we piloted new technologies (i.e. blockchain and smart contracts) to radically lower these transaction costs and provide the necessary transparency.

The starting point was a Proof-of-Concept developed by Rabobank, which was piloted on Bundles, a circular company that provides its customers with the service of 'clean laundry', by providing them a durable washing machine and charging them per washing cycle. The community of practice further developed the payment platform into the co-created Circular Service (CISE) Platform. The CISE platform functions as a decentralized digital administration system that adapts value management to circular ownership and incentive structures.

But how does this work? When the end-user washes his clothes, a payment is made in a virtual currency. This payment is automatically disbursed, through smart contracts, to not only Bundles, but to all the companies involved in operating the washing machine, service providers (e.g. Bundles), hardware providers (e.g. the manufacturer of the washing machine), but also consumable providers (e.g. washing detergent). This same model can be applied to all sorts of circular service networks, around various assets (e.g. CoffeeBundles, Pay-per-Km car sharing models, milk robots, et cetera.

The financier of the specific circular asset can also be included in the automatic disbursement of payments, thus being paid directly for the use (e.g. washing cycle) that his investment made possible. This way, financial repayments are based on performance, the unit of output, of the asset. This has the potential to create interesting hybrids of debt and equity. The incentive of the financier becomes aligned with the incentives of the service providers; to maintain the asset to operate.

This model can be scaled up, lowering the transaction costs to a negligible level, strongly increasing the attractiveness of investing in the circular economy in the most direct way, allowing for a relationship to be established between investors (also institutional investors) and the most innovative circular entrepreneurs.

A Commons-based Platform for Financial Data

In 2019, with the EU's Second Payment Service Directive (PSD2), the concept of open banking, already present in the UK, came to continental Europe. This will most probably lead to a rat race between financial institutions (e.g. the tech savvy big Dutch banks) and Big Tech-players (Amazon, Apple, Google etc.) to become the platform where everyone's financial data is gathered and analyzed. A single platform that through network effects and the sheer size of its database, will be able to outsmart all of its competitors, establishing itself as the new Google or Amazon of finance. It becomes 'the' portal to the people whose data is being analyzed - a position that brings unprecedented and extremely profitable possibilities for the gatekeeper which determines what connections being made and can demand kickbacks from every offer made to 'its' clients.

What this future looks like may be deduced from developments in other sectors such as Uber in the taxi market and Airbnb in accommodation. There the platform economy (in its early days often dubbed the 'sharing economy') has been hijacked by classical, if not turbo charged, capitalist corporations. Not 'sharing' is their motto, but strengthening and protecting their competitive position. With no voice, exit from the effective monopoly platform is the consumer's only 'choice'.

Alternative models have been, and are being, tried. However, in most sectors these have been initiated after the 'Wall Street platforms' had already established their network effect. Or they tried to prevent this in a time that the commercial platforms were generally seen as a revolutionary force for good.

That today, is different. Scandals have overwhelmed Big Tech in general (think of Facebooks privacy issues and fake news, Apple's tax avoidance, Amazon's labour rights issues, the competition fines in the EU for Google) and platforms in particular (Uber's charges ranging from sexism to underpayment of its drivers and the poor road safety track-record due to the long working hours). There is now a more fertile breeding ground for alternatives that respect privacy, operate transparently and operate in the interests of the user.

In this, the financial sector is a special case. There is not yet one single platform for managing financial services and data - if only because the regulation required has only just been realized. What may also hold back this development in finance, is the issue with trust and privacy for this particular data. However, traditional financial institutions have lost so much of this trust over the last decade that the appetite for an alternative is big.

What we envision is a platform that citizens can use to aggregate their financial data, allowing comparisons and analyses to achieve the goals they find worthwhile, to realize their values. It is thus not a corporation, not the market, that decides what happens, but rather the people themselves, in a conversation amongst themselves. In a cooperative model people can set the rules themselves, decide themselves on how the data can best be stored (minimizing the chance of data breaches), decide which other parties can access data and under what conditions. Advice from the analysis does not come from a black box and is not the result of an algorithm that focuses primarily on maximizing the financial interest of the intermediary. Advice can be personalized, mirroring personal preferences not just financially but also in social and ecological goals. So when you haven't thought about your energy supplier, and are probably paying more than needs to be the case, of the suggested alternatives not only the price but also their sustainability performance is indicated. This enables people to manage their matters in a more optimal way from a pure financial perspective, but also taking into account their other values.

With the support of the Porticus Foundation, the Finance and the Common Good program is being carried out in close collaboration between Socires and the SFL. SFL is a network of professors and academics of different universities in the Netherlands. Since 2009, SFL has proven itself by placing new financial reform themes on the agenda of the sector, regulators and policymakers. The planned activities are tried and tested recipes of both these organizations: think- and work tables, Communities of Practices, public evenings, seminars for young financiers and for today's decision makers, always including representatives from the state, market, financiers, scientists and social organizations. Through transformative meetings and conversations we build a shared problem definition and facilitate new connections which give birth to new solutions and methods.

1. World Cooperative Monitor 2018
https://monitor.coop/en

2. Toxopeus (2019) Financing sustainable innovation; From a principal-agent to a collective action perspective.

3. Financial Times, March 2017, Professional investors join the crowdfunding party
https://www.ft.com/content/235b5198-08ce-11e7-ac5a-903b21361b43

4. Achterberg (2019) The Circular Service Platform; A technical-administrative infrastructure for managing value in circular networks.

Concluding remarks

By Kees Buitendijk & Cor van Beuningen

IT IS A RATHER impossible task to recapitulate the contents of the 21 essays in this volume. They discuss a wide variety of topics from many different angles, and provide us with many new and profound perspectives on the issue of *Finance and the Common Good*. But, we don't stand surprised to see the scope of this volume's contents, as the title alone covers a lot of ground. Finance is a broad topic and *the common good* even more. However, compiling this volume was not always easy, because how should one go about uniting all these essays using a single theme? Although we have tried to group the essays using various categories, it is easy to see that (for example) the topics of FinTech, Chinese foreign policy and the future of the EU are areas of interest in their own right. However, it has also always been the goal to start a dialogue between many different voices, covering various topics, hailing from inside as well as outside the financial sector. This is because – as Jos van Gennip rightfully points out – there has been a lot of debate *about* the sector, but hardly ever a conversation *with* the sector. For that reason, we stand by Marshall McLuhan's famous adage that *'the medium is the message'*. Why? Because it is not only for of the contents of this volume that we value it; we also consider it an expression of the dialogue we believe to be so important. With this concern in mind, we believe that the notion of *Finance and the Common Good* – despite, or rather because of, the many topics it encompasses - is an adequate expression of the grand challenge we try to address. We only hope for this book to be a small step in the right way."

There are two concepts in particular that we think are worth repeating, as they surface in almost all of the essays in this volume. The first of these concepts is the phenomenon of *financialisation*. Although a broad notion, we find that financialisation is not merely an institutional, or even a formal, issue. It is not a 'simple' problem of the growth of *finance* vis-à-vis other economic activities. Financialisation encompasses the evolution of globalisation, technology, culture, and ethics, to name just a few topics. Even more fundamentally, financialisation is a matter of the (collective) human psyche: we have all been *financialised*. Financialisation is about *us*; it concerns *all of society*. The financial discourse has deeply permeated our thoughts, feelings, and expressions; our way of being-in-the-world. This means that 'de-financialisation' could never be only a matter of restoring the financial structures of the past. Wouter Bos highlights a similar problem in the context of (de-)globalisation: it seems to be utterly impossible. Our introduction referred to the saying 'what has been seen cannot be unseen': it will not do to simply revert to the structures that once were. For that reason, we stand with Pope Francis, who speaks of the *long, regenerative processes* that are necessary to develop a healthy (social and ecological) environment for the financial sector. Reforming finance does not begin with structural adjustments, but rather with the recalibration of our own thought processes. This brings us back to a simple question: who are we, and who do we want to be?

As we understand it, the quest for the self is always rooted in the subjects of place, culture, relations, and community. It is for this reason that we believe that the 'remedy' for financialisation can only be found in a concept that pays heed to all of these topics. The concept of the *Rhineland* is such a term. Even though this concept dates back several decades, it has only recently started to (re)generate attention. During the backlash of the financial crisis of 2008, many came to see the extent of the damage that pure Anglo-Saxon, or hyper-global, financial practices have wrecked on Western societies and economies. In the search for alternatives, memories of the Rhineland model started to appear. In the writings of Michel Albert and Soskice & Hall, among others, the tradition of the Rhineland stands for a characteristic North-Western European idea of societal and economic organization. However, and although easily overlooked, this tradition (as described by these authors) is far richer than economics alone: in the Rhineland explicit geographical conditions, cultural traits, and modes of societal interaction are displayed. Considering our *financialised* mode of being, we believe the initial rediscovery of the Rhineland should begin with the reassessment of these traits, conditions, interactions, and beliefs, because we doubt that the restoration of the classic Rhinelandic societal and economic constitution alone will prove a successful alternative to the current Anglo-Saxon financial monopolisation. If we do not have a proper understanding of our actual cultural, social, and societal dispositions, we lack a solid foundation for the reorientation of our economy. Any true attempt to uncover the ideal of Rhinelandic (financial) capitalism should therefore account for the aforementioned *long, regenerative process* (of re-relating) that precedes or accompanies it. However, especially when considering the current information-technological revolution overtaking the sector – with its profound impact on (all domains of) society – it is a fundamental and necessary study we should not evade.

As we have pointed out in our introduction but feel safe to repeat, this volume is a Socires initiative. The subject material perfectly bridges the topics of two of our programmes. Between 2015 and 2018, Socires ran its 'Ethics and Finance' programme, which included seminars, conferences, and round-table dialogues on many of the themes mentioned in this publication. All of the authors included in this volume contributed to the important (intellectual) work done in the three years of the programme. From 1 January 2019 onwards, we are involved in a new programme: 'Finance and the Common Good'. This time, Socires has joined forces with the renowned Sustainable Finance Lab (SFL), a research institute based at Utrecht University. This has led to a new team and a new name for the programme. More importantly, however, we have been able to draw on SFL's expertise to deepen our understanding of contemporary issues in and around the financial sector. In the months spent preparing the programme, we have found a mutual understanding of the complexity of the current financial-societal constitution, the belief that systemic change for the good is possible, and a shared motivation to contribute to a *Finance for the Common Good*. We look forward to continuing our work with this team.

Finally, some words of thanks are in order. We would like to thank Inge van der Bijl, Rixt Runia, and Rob Wadman, together with all their colleagues at Amsterdam University Press (AUP), for their great effort in producing this volume. Our praise goes to Michiel van Veluwen for the beautiful design, and to Tomas Buitendijk for proofreading and correcting the entire (!) book. A special word of thanks goes to our (former) colleagues at Socires, all of whom have been of great help in organizing the programme and/or preparing this volume: Wilma Bakker, Peter Broeders, Jos van Gennip, Hans Groen, and Wim Kuiper.

Of course, we are deeply indebted and owe our gratitude to the different authors in this volume. Without exception, they were keen to contribute when we asked them - and they have delivered essays that exceeded our expectations. All have gone to great lengths to provide us with insightful papers. We give full credit for the contents of the essays in this volume to their respective authors. All editorial mistakes that might surface are our own responsibility.

About the Contributors

JAN PETER BALKENENDE is the former Prime Minister and Minister of General Affairs of the Netherlands. He was Member of Parliament for the Christian Democratic Party (CDA) from 1998-2010, and party leader from 2001-2010. He is Professor of Governance, Institutions and Internationalisation at Erasmus University Rotterdam (EUR) and External Senior Advisor to EY.

COR VAN BEUNINGEN is senior advisor at Socires, where he co-coordinates different programmes. He holds Master's degrees in both Geography and Public Administration. In the past, he worked for the Dutch Ministry of Foreign Affairs, and had assignments in Colombia, Mauritania and Yemen. From 2000-2017 he was Director of Socires. He is known for his publications in different media, books and journals.

DIRK BEZEMER is Professor in the Economics of International Financial Development at the University of Groningen, where he teaches on banking, finance and the global monetary system. His published academic research, in part supported by the Institute for New Economic Thinking, is about the interrelations between financial development and economic growth, inequality, and resilience. He is a member of the Dutch Sustainable Finance Lab and was a co-writer for various WRR, OECD, World Bank and UNCTAD policy reports. Bezemer is an economics columnist for De Groene Amsterdammer and a regular contributor to Dutch and international media programmes and publications.

MAARTEN BIERMANS is an economist and philosopher. He works at the Rabobank where he is responsible for the bank's sustainable capital markets agenda. Furthermore, he is a lecturer at Tilburg University. He was co-author of the 2017 UN-Report on the Integration of the Sustainable Development Goals in Private Investment Agendas.

WOUTER BOS is former Minister of Finance and Deputy Prime Minister of the Netherlands (2007-2010). He was the leader of the Dutch Labour Party (PvdA) from 2002-2010. After that, he was partner at KPMG from 2010-2013. He has been Chairman of the Board of Directors at university hospital VUmc from 2013-2018. Currently, he is Chairman of the Invest-NL Foundation.

LANS BOVENBERG is Professor of Economics at Tilburg University, where he is engaged in a revision of economics education in Dutch high schools and is affiliated with the pension network Netspar. He also holds a chair on relational economics, values and leadership at Erasmus University of Rotterdam. He has previously been affiliated with the University of California in Berkeley, California, , the Dutch Ministry of Economic Affairs, the IMF in Washington DC, CPB in the Hague and the Dutch Social and Economic Council (SER).

GOVERT BUIJS holds the Abraham Kuyper Chair for Political Philosophy & Religion at the philosophy department of the Vrije Universiteit Amsterdam. Next to this, he also holds the Goldschmeding Research Chair 'Economics & Civil Society'. He teaches both in the Faculty of Humanities and in the School of Business and Economics of the VU. Buijs frequently acts as a policy advisor for (managers and boards of) non-profit and profit organisations in the Netherlands and is a regular commentator in Dutch media on socio-ethical issues.

KEES BUITENDIJK is the programme coordinator for the Finance and the Common Good project at Socires. He teaches at the Vrije Universiteit in Amsterdam, where he also carries out research on the philosophy of finance. He holds Master's degrees in both Philosophy and Public Administration.

SYLVESTER EIJFFINGER is Full Professor of Financial Economics and Jean Monnet Professor of European Financial and Monetary Integration at the Centre for Economic Research in the Department of Econo-mics at Tilburg University. He is also a Research Fellow at the Centre for

Economic Policy Research in London, UK and at the CESifo Research Network in Munich, Germany.

JOS VAN GENNIP is special advisor to the Socires Finance and the Common Good programme. He is a member of the Academic Council of the Wilfried Martens Centre for European Studies. In the past, he was Deputy Director General at the Ministry of Foreign Affairs in the Netherlands, Speaker on Foreign Relations for the Senate of the Netherlands, founder and first President of the Socires Foundation, and General Rapporteur for the political platform of the European People's Party (EPP).

JOHAN GRAAFLAND is Professor of Economics, Business and Ethics at Tilburg University. He is an economist and theologian specialising in the philosophy of economics, economic ethics, business ethics, corporate social responsibility, and the religion and economics debate. His research has been widely published in an array of international journals. He has written two volumes on the topic of Markets and Ethics. Between 2010-2013, he conducted a major research project on Corporate Social Responsibility in Europe, on behalf of the European Union. From 2017 onwards he is heading together with Govert Buijs a research project on "What good markets are good for" on behalf of Templeton World Charity Foundation, Inc.

WOPKE HOEKSTRA is the Minister of Finance of the Kingdom of the Netherlands.

EELKE DE JONG is Professor of International Economics at Radboud University. He is currently involved with the 2017-2020 research group 'Moral Markets – What Good Markets Are Good for', for which he is doing research on cultural differences and economic cooperation within Europe. Furthermore, he is deputy chair of the Board of the Thijmgenootschap and honorary member of the Scientific Advisory Board of Ordo socialis, https://ordosocialis.de/en/wissenschaftlicher-beirat/.

THEODOR KOCKELKOREN is Inspector General of the Dutch Mining Authority. From 2002-2015, he was affiliated with the Dutch Authority for Financial Markets (AFM). In the final few years of his involvement with AFM, he was member of the board of directors. He was a partner at McKinsey, and was also the chair of the G20/OECD taskforce on Financial Consumer Protection.

ROLAND KUPERS is an advisor on Complexity, Resilience and Energy Transition, as well as an Associate Researcher at the Institute for Advanced Studies at the University of Amsterdam. A theoretical physicist by training, Roland spent a decade each at AT&T and at Shell in various senior executive functions, including Vice President for Sustainable Development and Vice President Global LNG. He has published widely, including in HBR, on Project Syndicate and co-authored The Essence of scenarios (AUP 2014), Complexity and the art of public policy (PUP 2014) and Turbulence: A corporate perspective on collaborating for resilience (AUP 2014). He is also the managing director of NewEconomicMetrics BV, a fintech start-up.

CARLA MOONEN is president of the Royal Dutch Association of Engineers. She is a member of the Executive Committee of the Confederation of Netherlands Industry and Employers. Next to this she is candidate Senator. Earlier, she was Senior Adviser to the Cabinet of the Dutch Prime Minister (2008-2013) and Deputy Director of the Government Finance Inspectorate. From 2013-2017 she served as Chair of the Brabantse Delta Water Authority Board. From 2017 till 2019 she was Chairperson of the Pension Fund for the Care and Welfare Sector. She studied Land- and Watermanagement, Economics and Environmental Economy.

HERMAN VAN ROMPUY was President of the European Council from 2009 to 2014. Before this period, he was among other things the Minister of Budget, a Senator, and the Prime Minister (from 2008 to 2009) of Belgium. Since September 2015, he is Chairman of the European Policy Centre.

HAROON SHEIKH is senior researcher at the Dutch Scientific Council for Government Policy (WRR). Before he was Head of Research at Dasym Investment Strategies and he led the European think-tank FreedomLab. He is a member of staff at the Ethos Centre for research and education at the Vrije Universiteit, Amsterdam. He has published in various national and international media like Foreign Affairs, The Financial Times and Het Financieel Dagblad and he is a regular contributor to NRC Handelsblad. His first book 'De Opkomst van het Oosten' ('The Rise of the East') was published in 2016. His most recent book, 'Embedding Technopolis', was published in the fall of 2017. In the course of 2019, his book on 'Hydropolitics' will appear.

RENS VAN TILBURG is director of the Sustainable Finance Lab. With the SFL members, a network of 20 academics from different Dutch universities and the SFL-secretariat at Utrecht University, he develops new ideas for a more stable and sustainable financial sector and provides a platform to discuss these with the financial sector, supervisors, policy makers and other stakeholders.

STEVEN VANACKERE is the former Flemish Minister of Welfare, Family and Public Health (2007-2008), Belgian Federal Deputy Prime Minister and Minister of the Civil Service, Public Enterprise and Institutional Reform (2008-2009), Deputy Prime Minister and Minister of Foreign Affairs and Institutional Reform (2009-2011) and Federal Deputy Minister and Minister of Finance (2011-2013). Until January 2019, he was a senator for the Belgian political party CD&V.

CHRISTIAAN VOS is a fiscal economist and philosopher. He works at the Dutch Central Bank (De Nederlandsche Bank) as senior policy advisor on capital requirements and he is lecturer Ethics and Methodology of Taxation at the University of Amsterdam. He has been a tax adviser for more than 25 years and has published regularly on ethics and taxation.